THE PATHLESS LAND

JOYCE COLLIN-SMITH

A SEQUEL TO CALL NO MAN MASTER

Visit us online at www.authorsonline.co.uk

An AuthorsOnLine Book

Published by Authors OnLine Ltd 2003

Copyright © 2003 Authors OnLine Ltd
Text Copyright © 2003 Joyce Collin-Smith
Cover © 2003 Paul Stanney

The moral right of the author has been asserted

All rights reserved. No part of this publication may be reproduced, stored in a retrieval system, or transmitted in any form or by any means, electronic, mechanical, photocopy, recording or otherwise, without prior written permission of the copyright owner. Nor can it be circulated in any form of binding or cover other than that in which it is published and without similar condition including this condition being imposed on a subsequent purchaser

Paperback ISBN 0-7552-0095-0

Authors OnLine Ltd
15-17 Maidenhead Street
Hertford SG14 1DW
England

This book is also available in e-book format from
www.authorsonline.co.uk

For
JOHNNY FINCHAM
Good friend and supportive colleague for many years.

My grateful thanks are due to

PAUL STARLING for a great deal of help in preparing the manuscript and dealing with problems.

GREGORY VLAMIS for much time-consuming researching and advice.

ALISON BRIGHT for encouragement and typing of first tapes.

Especial thanks to
PAUL STANNEY
for his great kindness in designing the book cover

'That element of tragedy which lies in the very fact of frequency, has not yet wrought itself into the coarse emotion of mankind; and perhaps our frames could hardly bear much of it. If we had a keen vision and feeling of all ordinary human life, it would be like hearing the grass grow and the squirrel's heartbeat, and we should die of that roar which lies on the other side of silence.

Middlemarch
George Elliot

CHAPTERS

PROLOGUE   vi

The Other Side of Silence

1. The Pathless Land   1
2. The Crystal Kingdom   18
3. Elements and Elementals   33
4. If Gaia is Mother who is Father?   48
5. Angels and Archangels   69
6. Working with the Senses   90
7. 'To sleep perchance to dream'   104
8. Pathways of the Ancients   116
9. The Magic of Numbers   131

Tools and Techniques

10. Working with the Tarot   145
11. The Qualities of Time (Astrology)   164
12. The Tree of Life (Cabala)   186
13. The Way of the Carpenter   199

EPILOGUE   212

Bibliography   214

Index   217

PROLOGUE

I had sat at the feet of too many Masters.

Now in retirement, I seem to have come full circle. The disciplines of Gurdjieff and Ouspensky Work; the laughing charm of Maharishi Mahesh Yogi; the strange, psychic power of the Indonesian mystic Pak Subuh; even the simple, straightforward Christianity of Frank Buchman, founder of the Moral Rearmament, have given me experience of different ways of looking for the Truth.

But it has come increasingly apparent to me that the way of knowledge and understanding is not somewhere 'out there', to be found through the words of masters, however wise and experienced they might be. The Way seems to be individual to each person, and the search for it, the efforts to find it, may be, paradoxically, themselves the Way.

It is a long time since I used to sit in the corner of the library at school reading Rudolf Steiner and pausing to gaze out of the windows over the spires and cupolas of Oxford, deep in thought. Amazed by the realisation that there might be other modes of consciousness, even other worlds, I would ask myself 'who am I?'

The intense longing to know the meaning of life, to know God, has been with me always. I was scarcely out of school when I encountered the Oxford Group, as MRA was then called. I started eagerly on the practices Dr. Buchman introduced to the young people of both City and University. But it was not very long before I realised that the tenets of Absolute Honesty, Absolute Purity, Absolute Unselfishness and Absolute Love, which we were supposed to know, were as hopelessly beyond reach as flying to the Moon. I also became uneasy with the 'Listening to God' technique, which Buchmanites practised twice a day. Writing down the messages from God was easy--there were always plenty! But they began to seem suspiciously like my own inventions.

Like my father, grandfather and great-grandfathers before me, I became a journalist. The experience of covering and reporting people's completely opposing and deeply held convictions at meetings of organisations or political parties, and witnessing the anger that underlies so much of human life and intercourse, brought me to rapid realisation of certain worldly problems.

I then faced war circumstances as a WAAF intelligence officer, married when in the service; divorced; and returned to Fleet Street as a single mother with a little daughter to support. Back in the newspaper world, I made my second, most happy marriage, and through my husband Richard (Derry) Collin-Smith, I met Rodney Collin, who was Derry's brother. Best known now as the author of *The Theory of Celestial Influence, The Theory of Eternal Life* and other books, he was a pupil and close associate of P.D.Ouspensky.

The whole Gurdjieff/Ouspensky field of ideas awakened an enormously enthusiastic response in me. I was soon off to Mexico to visit Rodney's group and to learn at his feet. He was my mentor for some years until his strange death at the age of only 48. From Rodney Collin I toook readily to the idea that Mankind is a self-evolving species, but that much greater efforts than 'listening to God' are needed to awaken our latent possibilities.

On returning to London, I was accepted into the rather closed Society for the Study of Normal Man, (later renamed Normal Psychology), inheritors of the group that had studied with Ouspensky himself until his death--people whom Rodney had known. I worked diligently but became disillusioned after some years. I thought there was a 'we are the Chosen People' atmosphere which cut the Ouspenskyites off from ordinary contacts in life, and that there was a tendency to repeat Ouspensky and Gurdjieff teaching parrot fashion, not developing anything in themselves.

When Pak Subuh came to London, some of the Ouspensky people dabbled with his practice known as the Latihan--Indonesian for the Exercise. The effects were powerful, but appeared to me to be more psychic rather than spiritual. I was not happy with the results I experienced in myself and witnessed in other aspirants

Fate brought me inevitably into contact with Maharishi Mahesh Yogi. Meeting him in the early days when he had not yet achieved the vast following he had later, I was in the interesting position of driving him around in my car, working in his household in Prince Albert Road, Regent Park, and being initiated into his practice of Transcendental Meditation by the Master himself. In later years I have felt that spiritual and psychological teachers are of enormous help to anyone who honestly searches for the Truth. Gurus who demand a total commitment have their dangers.

But whatever fate may bring, in the long run only committed personal efforts to achieve understanding seem to bring development and advancement. In this New Age, much ancient knowledge which was regarded as suspect because of its esoteric nature is becoming available to everyone who desires it. I have garnered some of it for those who feel they are traveling a lonely path, and who ask themselves the eternal questions common to mankind.

1

The Pathless Land

There are three basic questions which in times of uncertainty or despondency, most people ask themselves inwardly: 'Who am I?' 'What am I supposed to be doing?' and 'What do I want?' and having turned to books, to self appointed teachers and ancient Masters and considered their many words, perhaps put them aside with the thought that there is no answer anywhere to the deepest questions that life poses.

Truth is a 'pathless land' as the Indian mystic Krishnamurti said. And yet many people do seem to walk that land with confidence of knowing something, of knowing about higher worlds than this one, other modes of consciousness, discarnate beings, Angels and the gods. And many seem to feel that they know what mankind may be and our purpose and possibilities on this earth.

So how can I begin to equip myself for a journey into that pathless land, when I can't even find a signpost which doesn't swing in the wind this way and that, pointing in one direction or another and back again?

The Austrian philosopher Rudolf Steiner who died in 1928, begins his great classic tome of a book 'Knowledge of the Higher Worlds and its Attainment' with this question. He was very verbose. He was a Victorian writer to a large extent in his attitude. A great many words were used where we would think less would do. He produced many heavy books, and people don't find him easy to read these days. But he had the most remarkable range of acquired knowledge which still has a bearing on medical matters, educational matters, and agricultural matters, today. He is not often quoted now, but his rather interesting remark, made in the 1920s that 'if you feed herbivorous animals with carnivorous matter, they will go mad,' was quoted in the House of Commons during the outbreak of spongiform encephalitis--the so-called 'mad cow disease'. Feeding sheeps' brains to cattle was of course believed to be a primary cause of the disease in which the animals stumbled about and appeared 'mad.'

Steiner had no master. He was self taught and he held very strongly the view that the truth not only lies within oneself, but that all that is needed for an individual person to find his way in life is to begin to look within. If he is fortunate he may encounter the help, not of a master to whom he must commit himself with absolute trust, but somebody who has gone some distance further along the path and who can therefore be counted on as a friend. Dr. Steiner found several friends, but he was essentially a lone traveller. With the aid of such a friend, however, a traveller can make a beginning on the Way. Once an aspirant begins to feel motivated and wants to take responsibility for his/her own development, then help of this sort from time to time is probably all that is needed.

Making a Beginner's Mind!

I'm hoping that this book may prove of value to people who have cast aside many heavier works and who just want a little assistance to get going. It follows *Call No Man Master*, which tells of my days with the Maharishi Mahesh Yogi; with Pak Subuh the Indonesian mystic; in Mexico with Rodney Collin and the followers of Ouspensky, etc. I am in my mid-eighties so I have gathered a few ideas of my own, which may be useful, as a widely travelled 'friend' to those who look for one at this time.

It could be a good idea to cultivate what's rather charmingly been called a 'beginner's mind'. That is to come innocently to ideas which may be new or may be not acceptable to you, but which, if they're just taken on board for the moment can be pointers for something which may be of value later on.

There's a strong tendency to want all knowledge to fit into one's own pre-conceived views, or what one has picked up along the way. And sometimes people have a line of thought, a belief, a tradition, from childhood or the home background, or something already examined and perhaps partially discarded and yet remaining as a basis of their personal thought. This can be a stumbling block. The package of thought may need to fit into a much wider field of knowledge, before it can actually be useful in helping you to go forward.

Of course, we don't know for certain who we are, or what our potential is, or what life is or where we came from, or where we may be going, or what really is beyond the material level of this world. There are no ready made answers, no written answers anywhere that really satisfy us all. But self-understanding can begin to grow, people can begin to say, 'I see now what it is about - what I must be about in this life'. But to get to the point where one begins to see, a certain amount of effort is needed.

This book is intended to help those who are willing and want to make efforts, not super-human efforts, nor efforts of asceticism or starvation or rigorous rituals of any kind but simply every day continuous efforts towards growth of consciousness. And that's why, at the end of every chapter, there will be some indication of what you might do before moving on -- and indeed continue to do as a background to your thoughts.

First There Was Energy

We have to begin somewhere so we will begin with the basic concept that there is surely a First Cause, a Creator, God, the Absolute, the godhead, whatever we want to call it. The first cause *could* be just energy -- if we go along with the Big Bang Theory which is fashionable today: energy exploding outwards forming the first primordial soup, then gaseous clouds solidifying into matter and the physical universe. And so forming, the physical universe may have carried with it something which we could call the Spirit. Without some such concept there would only be eternal chaos and none of the beauty of created things. Perhaps that is an acceptable idea to most people who start reading this book? Of course many people say the first cause might be Love and they tend to feel that love is the highest experience which we are capable of having and that this is, therefore, a reflection of God. But we can't actually prove that the first cause is love. Love might be a man-made concept. Ordinary love between people and in our everyday dealings with others, may be just the currency with which we work to 'pay the bills' of every day living. The currency of this world. But the word Love can of course be expressive of the essence of something very much bigger. However we can't prove that love is the first cause, but we can prove to our satisfaction, at least scientifically, that energy is.

To develop understanding, it is necessary to work a bit. Higher knowledge can't be handed out on a plate. There can be a great tendency to say 'I know' when we only mean 'I believe'. So test all statements in this book, test your own understanding, and test me and what I say. Then we can begin to differentiate between scientific fact, and ideas and theories -- or mere fantasies -- and find what is acceptable to you, yourself.

Occult and Esoteric Knowledge

We need to have a look at an enormous field of knowledge, including occult and esoteric knowledge. Occult has nothing spooky about it as sometimes people seem to think. Occult simply means that which is hidden. The Sun is in a state of occultation when the clouds are in front of it. And esoteric, a word frequently used and often not understood means that which comes from the core centre. Exoteric means the ordinary outer things of this world and esoteric means the core.

To grow in understanding we should not be spending all our time just thinking about theoretical knowledge, either psychological or metaphysical, scientific or spiritual. All this is needed. But we also need practical experience of the occult and esoteric worlds. Judaic law said *'The teaching is impotent without experience and the experience is unfulfilled without the teaching.'* Therefore we need both.

There's an old army saying 'Tell me and I'll forget, show me and I'll remember, let me do it and I'll understand'. And this of course, I'm stressing, because of the great importance of being willing to *do* something in order to make one's own pathway through that pathless land. We need to learn to use certain tools, such as intelligence and discrimination, to grow in consciousness. Doing this is to open pathways in the brain.

Madame H.P. Blavatsky, the founder of the Theosophical Society, in the Nineteenth Century, believed very strongly that it was possible to make new pathways that could be physically found in the brain. These would make greater self-knowledge and understanding possible. Of course at the moment we have very little understanding of the complex organism known as the brain, and what the human mind may be. It is as useless to think that one could find the 'mind' by dissecting the brain as it would be to dissect the body in order to find the soul. The soul is not there to be seen in the physical form. But nevertheless the brain, which simply looks like a lot of strange, tightly-folded grey-white tubes, and which is divided into two halves -- the left and right brain hemispheres -- really has many more possibilities than we know about.

In recent years, the Maharishi Mahesh Yogi, founder of The Spiritual Regeneration Movement, which introduced TM, initiated some experiments with doctors who were his followers, attaching electrodes to the heads of people who were in deep 'transcendental meditation' and came to the conclusion that it is possible that genuine physical changes could be made: at least there were, apparently, electronic impulses that could be detected when people were in a state of meditation. So it might be that we really have to open channels in the brain, and not only open them but keep them open, if we are to develop and realise our potential.

The Automatic Pilot

The strange Caucasian Greek teacher G.I. Gurdjieff who died on October 29th, 1949, spoke a great deal about man's potential. He said that mankind was like a house wired for electricity but he didn't know how to switch on the light, so he went around groping in a few small rooms by the light of a candle not knowing that he had many great chambers -- probably one leading to another and further yet -- in the enormous mansion that is his. We just go on living in the very small surroundings that are familiar to us.

To grow in consciousness we need to start observing. We need to start by observing ourselves, and for this purpose Gurdjieff's exercises, one of which is known as self-remembering, are extremely useful. We spend very much of our time in a kind of dopey, waking sleep, living on a sort of automatic pilot. The automatic pilot seems very helpful, otherwise we expend an awful lot of energy doing things which we don't need to do with our full attention.

The observation of the automatic pilot is useful in everyday things like driving a car, typing, using a word processor, housework, using a washing machine. When you are learning to drive, full attention is put on the gears, the brake, the mirror, the steering -- all the many functions that have to be put together and understood in order to be safe in one's own car. For quite a long time it seems almost impossible that it will ever be clear how to use all those functions together in harmony. After a certain while, driving a car becomes easy and the automatic pilot takes over. Now when driving, the automatic pilot can do it and you can talk to the friend sitting beside you, watch the traffic, the dog crossing the road in front of you, wave to a friend you see and be in a perfectly safe state behind the wheel. But in a real emergency it is necessary to wake up so that the full conscious mind comes into play and deals with the situation. This we can do because it is a 'natural' function to come fully awake in such a moment.

The same thing applies if we are using a word processor and typing fast. If you stop and think to yourself 'where is the letter "g" ?' or 'where is the semi-colon?' you may be surprised to find that you don't seem to know where these keys are. It is only your fingers that know. You wiggle your fingers and find the letter "g" or the semi-colon. Automatic pilot has long taken over and enables you to rattle along at speed. All the everyday things done at home, tend to be done on automatic pilot and we save our energy by this means. But to be able to come fully awake and to use the conscious mind at any time, is not only very important but it is part of growth of understanding of our possibilities.

The plant kingdom seems to live on 'automatic pilot' all the time, and the lower animals very largely so. The higher animals seem to have a greater degree of consciousness. But we alone can actually *decide* to 'wake up', to be aware of ourselves and of our possible role. So the first thing may be to wake up and try to find out what Mankind actually is. And how to sustain and increase our creative energy by our own actions.

Energy Leaks Out

We need to look inward, at ourselves, to avoid what Gurdjieff called negative emotions. That is, continually feeling the down drag of that which we don't like, grumbling to ourselves, analyzing our depression, inwardly talking to ourselves about the unhappy experiences we have had, people we dislike, or anything that is not satisfyingly good in our lives at the moment. Negative emotions make enormous leaks in energy, so feeling perpetually tired is one of the signs of somebody who lives on automatic pilot and who gives full play to negative emotions without noticing what is happening. To avoid these leaks in energy, we need to watch ourselves, and we need to look outward to observe the world around us as well. Sometimes we can be surprised by a childlike wonder if we really look at the world around us, and see and appreciate the recurrent cycles of night and day, the seasons, growth, maturity, procreation, death. What a Mind there must be behind all created things.

We have in ourselves many different 'I's and the lack of unity within us makes for one of our big problems! For instance we are all familiar with going to bed at night and saying 'I will get up at 6 o clock in the morning and do my exercises', or 'finish my work'. But at 6 o clock in the morning that 'I' which made the inner promise, just doesn't happen to be around any more and the 'I' that wakes up thinks it would be all right to have another half hour in bed! It is part of our human nature that we are very fragmented and there are many different opposing 'I's that we may be familiar with. The 'I' dealing with our intimate family may be rather different from the 'I' that does a day's work in the office. We know that we often present a different side of ourselves to different people and under different circumstances.

We can't change this easily, but it is well worth watching and being aware of when we put on a special voice or a different way of speaking or dress in a different way to be with different people. Just observe it. This is the 'I' that wants to be smart and chic and up to date, and this is the 'I' that wants to relax at home and doesn't care how I look. This is the 'I' that wants to be known to my parents, or to my children. I may have a different 'I' for my partner. There would certainly be a different 'I' at the breakfast table, from the 'I' who was in bed with a lover last night! You will see that you present different sides of yourself under different circumstances. Observe this as you observe other aspects of your daily life, you will find it all helps towards self knowledge. Is there a real and constant 'I' at all?

A World of Ideas

Through ideas come visions, visualisation, and metaphysical notions. Physics is a study of the interplay of energy and matter, knowledge of physical phenomena. Metaphysics is seeking the inner meaning by visionary means.

All these ideas that I am talking about, are of course, philosophical ideas. People sometimes think that philosophy means the study of some dry as dust system or ideology such as Existentialism or Logical Positivism or Dialectical Materialism -- those Nineteenth Century philosophies. Or some other theory about how we ought to live or how society ought to be run!

But philosophy was originally in two parts: natural philosophy, which is the study of physical phenomena of all kinds; and moral philosophy which is the ethics and beliefs arising from what we observe. So let's observe.

On this earth there are many levels of organic life from simple living organisms up to mankind. Below us there is the mineral realm, slow moving, perfect in its own way. And above us........ What? Many levels of discarnate beings? It's said by psychics that there are many, many angels and very few of us -- very few humans. Mankind is perhaps just a small stratum of existence. Who knows? These ideas are worth pondering on. But let's not say, we know, but simply we are thinking about it.

Somewhere between the heavy vibrations of energy in the mineral realm and the high, high rapid vibrations of the angels, we, humankind -- little men/little women -- seem to fit in. Just a small slot, perhaps, in a long chain of mutually dependent and interdependent creatures: like cog wheels. We are all creatures of the Creator. Of course, the word creation is the root word from which springs Creator, creativity, and creature. So if we are children of the Creator, creatures of the creator, we must in our very nature be creative too. This we need to learn, to make use of in order to grow up.

In the book of Genesis, there is the strange legend, myth, of God making the World in seven days and the garden 'Eastward in Eden'. This is just a way of explaining something in mythological terms. God made Man 'in his own image' we are told. So according to this story, there must be a creator god who made mankind to have free will like Himself. So mankind, alone on this earth, is able to understand a concept -- the concept of good and evil, for instance. The animals don't have anything like the same degree of free will as we do and the plants have no free will at all. They just have the will to live and grow. Lower levels of life have very little free will and just accept their circumstances.

Understanding a Concept

We, humankind, can decide whether to accept or reject the circumstances we find ourselves in; to choose whether we will try to get out, or try and change things for the better. Whether we will nurture and protect and care for those lower species who are, in very many ways, at our mercy. Or whether to exploit them, or even destroy them. It says in Genesis that we were made, not only in the image of God, but 'to have dominion over all the other creatures of the earth'. We may not like the idea of having dominion over the other creatures of the earth. But if we can understand more than they can, because we can understand the concept of what is good and what is bad: and if we have more of an ability to move around freely and to decide whether to accept or reject, then it is obviously within the boundaries of our possibility, that we can help to nurture and sustain all the species that are simpler than ourselves, and that live on this earth with us. And to help and protect and nurture and sustain the earth itself.

There is an old tradition, recently much to the fore again, that calls the earth Gaia the earth mother; a living being in her own right. We are her children, fed by her, sustained by her and nevertheless needing to protect our mother. This is a very ancient basic concept, nowadays rather popular, and I'm sure that the growing interest in ecology is much linked up with this ancient knowledge coming to the fore at the present time. Let's protect the earth and not pollute the seas and not cause damage wherever we go is the mindset of the New Age.

The American geologist Ra Bonewitz, who is also a mystic, puts many of these ideas very well when he says 'We are sons and daughters of the cosmos, children of the stars.' He points out that there is nothing in us which is not in the stars.

The human body is certainly made from the elements available here, and our life on this earth is sustained by these elements. They are the basics that we can actually exist with. The air-mixture, (the gases), that we can breathe without being suffocated or poisoned, exist with this earth. On the moon or in outer space, astronauts can't breath unaided. The amount of heat that we need comes from our sun, round which we are in constant orbit. It's much too cold or too hot for us on other planets. We should freeze or fry. The rain water, the solid foods and the minerals of which our bones and our bodies are made, all keep us alive and kicking. But there seems to be something in us that is more than the elements. Pythagoras (sixth century BC), by tradition said 'I am a child of earth and of starry heaven. But my race is of heaven.' The idea that there is more to us than the body goes back very far in time.

When Ra Bonewitz speaks of minerals he speaks particularly of crystals, which interest people very much nowadays. He points out that we tend to think of minerals as the lowest point of energy because of their slow vibration. But seen from the standpoint of the evolution of the universe, the mineral kingdom was formed under the highest energy conditions and therefore represents the highest energy to which man can attune. 'These energies carry the very imprint of the creation of the Universe and we need to align ourselves with the same creative impulse, the so-called thought in the mind of God that appears to be the motivation of the Universe,' Bonewitz says. 'Man is a synthesis of matter and spirit within himself, a being of spirit encased in a body of matter which is a perfect microcosm of the universe itself, the divine being whose body is the universe. This synthesis is part of the evolution, not only of man, but also of the earth itself. Maybe we are here, not simply with the idea of trying to get out or get back to the source, not just to escape from matter into spirit, but to see how to reach up into spirit and to bring spirit down into the denser realms, to infuse matter with spirit.'

Remembering Ourselves

These are very wide ideas of what we might think about in the sense of a universe formed from energy, thrusting outwards in the first instance, solidifying into matter and bringing into natural creation many species of being. We ourselves, humankind, slot in somewhere and seem to have some purpose.

I have made a lot of this idea that we need to observe ourselves and not just read a book and think of a few ideas, but try to make them real for ourselves. So we need some practices that we can do. The first one I suggest is an adaptation of Gurdjieff's self-remembering. Let's start thinking of that as being the first thing to get under way and to continue doing for a long time. Indeed we can do it all our lives with benefit.

To start self-remembering the first time, sit in a comfortable position: not necessarily in a real meditation posture, but simply where you can be conscious of your body, your seat on a chair, clothes on your body and what you can feel of your body itself. Then begin to use all five of the senses.

The first of the senses is sight. With eyes wide open, take in everything that you can see around you now in this moment: the room, furniture, any other people, anything through the window. Casting your thoughts wider, remind yourself where you are: in this house, in this town, in this place, in this time, in this country, in this Western hemisphere, in this world. This world is our planet earth which is turning on its own axis every 24 hours and spiralling with the other planets around our sun making our solar system. And our sun, with all the attendant planets spirals along our own path, within our galaxy the Milky Way. On a starry night you can see the Milky Way: that broad white band overhead which looks like a white rainbow across the heavens, only wider. It looks like a rainbow because it is really a spiral and we are in the other side of what we can see. Looking out, we are looking into the spiral of this enormous galaxy which is millions of stars. This galaxy is itself only one of the many galaxies within this universe -- so how very tiny we are! Feel this......and then return to where you are sitting in the room with this book on your lap.

When you are doing self-remembering you don't have to go through all of the above every time! But be aware of where you are relative to other things. Then use the other senses:

Hearing: what can you hear? There is nearly always something to be heard . In a town there is traffic noise. There may be voices, a dog barking, a radio or TV in the distance. In the country, maybe there is only the sound of the wind in the trees or the birds singing. Sometimes there's real utter silence. But not very often. Use your hearing: stretch it and really hear anything that is audible.

Use your sense of smell. Flare your nostrils in the way a

cat, dog, horse can flare their nostrils to pick up any scent. What can you smell? Now in this moment. Sometimes there are very pleasant scents or smells, sometimes very subtle ones; at other times there may be something unpleasant that we don't want from another person or something we don't like. Be conscious, simply be conscious of what you smell.

Taste: unless you are eating, you don't generally taste anything but as taste and smell are so closely linked if you open your mouth it is possible that you can get a sort of taste/smell.

Touch: with your hands, what can you touch? Clothes, the chair, anything within reach.

With seeing, hearing, smelling, tasting, touching -- all those five senses -- bring yourself into a state of real alertness and hold it for as long as you can. Do it repeatedly.

There are, of course, higher senses but it is quite enough at the moment if we start using consciously the five lower senses that we take so much for granted but through which all our experience of normal things on this world is filtered. By repeating this exercise you will find that you come into a greater state of alertness. Soon you will have no need to sit down in a chair and prepare yourself to do it. Do it anywhere, any time. Bring yourself into a state of acute awareness of the circumstances and surroundings -- and yourself there, in that moment of time . But you will not be able to hold the state of conscious awareness for very long.

An Experiment in Self-Remembering

When the Russian philosopher, P D Ouspensky, who was a pupil of Gurdjieff, was first given this exercise by Gurdjieff himself in St. Petersburg (about 1912), he thought it would be very easy to 'remember himself' and bring himself into a state of continual alertness and awareness of what is going on. He recalls in his book, 'In Search of the Miraculous', how he went out on foot along the Nevski Prospekt which is a boulevard running alongside the River Neva in that city. He walked along, looking at the horses and carriages going along the road, at the river flowing and the steamers and other boats on the river, at the houses, at everything that could be seen. He felt the cold air, listened to all the sounds and experienced everything in a very alive way, happy that he was self-remembering! About an hour and a half later, in his apartment back home, he suddenly realised with a great jolt, that he had gone onto automatic pilot (although of course that word was not known at that time) and had gone into a state of waking sleep and remembered nothing more, except in that sleepy, dreamy way. He remembered that he had called at the tobacconist who made his special cigarettes and that he had ordered some more. He had gone to the stationers and bought some pens, he had called on a friend to pick up a book and then returned home. But he had not 'remembered himself' at all, after the first few moments.

You will find the same thing. It sounds very easy but it is, in fact, very difficult to do self remembering for more than a few moments. You will be lucky if you succeed in doing it for more than a minute or two. But try and repeat and repeat and try again and again.

Thinking in terms of the leaks of energy through negative emotions, try to be awake to yourself in any moment of annoyance, anger, irritation: all those negative things that we all experience so frequently. If we are caught in a traffic snarl-up and are going to be late for an appointment, we are all familiar with how difficult it is to remain calm. You may want to sound your horn and express your anger. This is when your energy will be draining away. If you can notice this happening and stop it, you will find that, instead of arriving at your appointment late and very flustered, you will arrive late but calm -- which is very much better. So watching negative emotions and observing what is happening enables one to stop it occasionally.

We can't always stop negative emotions. Sometimes anger

may be quite justifiable and very human. I am not suggesting that we try to change ourselves overnight. But let's just observe and watch what is happening; watch when you experience these things and you will find you have more energy at the end of the week. If you catch yourself in a state of negative emotion and remember yourself by thinking 'Who am I?' 'Where am I?' 'What is this?' You will find that you are calmer, that life is more interesting and more positive and more worthwhile.

Not long ago I was reclining in a sunlounger under trees in my garden, working on the manuscript of this book. I glanced up and saw that a tiny, green, winged insect was sitting on my bare toe. It was delicate and fine as gossamer as it hovered there. I was filled with amazement as I watched this tiny life - - so small, and yet presumably having some sensual perception, a need to eat, the ability to digest its food; some sort of reproductive system that enables its species to procreate. My moment of wonder was not dissimilar to experiences of early childhood, when every creature, every observed circumstance, filled me with amazement and delight. Now that I am well into my eighties and can't get about much, life seems strangely simplified. Sometimes the childhood innocence and delight return. And yet over how many years of vigorous living, have insects seemed to be just creepy-crawlies or tiresome fluttery things to be brushed aside with casual inattention. I found myself in that moment remembering the words of Francis Thompson:

'The angels keep their ancient places,
Turn but a stone and start a wing'
Tis you, tis your estranged faces
That miss the many-splendoured thing.....'

How little we appreciate the marvels and the extraordinary beauty of creation as we rush round busily doing things.

Pointers on the Way

In a way, the ideas that I am suggesting, are simply pointers for anyone who wants to step out into that pathless land with the thought that you will be able ultimately to make your way forward relatively easily, because you will know more about yourself, your own nature, what you can do and what you can become. But we all have to make our own way.

It's rather as though each of us needs to sink a bore hole in that land to draw up the water to sustain us in any temporary resting place. We each have to have our own bore hole down into the waters. And we all have a different type of container. The one with a red plastic bucket may feel the water that is drawn up is different from the water drawn up in somebody else's old white enamel pail, or a galvanised container, or a silver champagne bucket! The water is always the same because the bore hole leads down into the well of the waters of eternal life. But the vessel may carry its own impurities. Even a golden bowl needs to be spotlessly clean, and that is not always possible. We carry the impurities of our own many preconceived notions and experiences. But all the same, let's dip into the waters, refresh ourselves and do our best.

Suggested Exercises.

1. Ask yourself the questions: 'Who am I?' 'What am I supposed to be doing?' 'What do I want?'

2. Do the exercise of self-remembering every time it occurs to you, if possible, several times a day.

3. Watch the leaks of energy through negative emotions. Stop them and consider their nature.

2

The Crystal Kingdom

There was a time some years ago when I ran a crystal group. I didn't start with the idea of organizing or running a crystal group. I was simply asked to invite to my house a number of people who wanted to join the 'networking' that Sir George Trevelyan, founder of the Wrekin Trust, was then launching. The idea was that people of like mind, who wanted to grow in consciousness, should gather in separate houses and work together in some way. When I was given a list of names of people, some of whom I didn't know and hadn't worked with before, I was very willing that they should come. But I thought, 'what are we going to talk about?' So I put a few crystals on a round table to make a focal point and get the conversation going. And from that, grew what we later called the Crystal Tea Party! We met once a month, and people took to bringing their own crystals, and putting them on the low, central table where I put my own crystals on display. This was in a sitting room overlooking the river, in the country house in Norfolk where my husband and I lived.

More and more crystals would come and be taken away again, and it was almost as though we had a whole orchestra or crystals -- all vibrating on their own wavelengths--and very powerful indeed it seemed to become. It was lovely, very beautiful, and people were very pleased with it. But gradually I came to realise that people were coming to almost worship these crystals as if they were little gods. They didn't want to hear about anything else other than the beauty of the crystals, and they began to be very sure that they could heal all ailments if they knew the difference between one and the other. They considered the possibility we could heal almost anything from arthritis to toothache by getting the right crystal!

I began to lose interest in this experiment. It might of course be true that if we spent years really studying the different crystals we would find out there is a tendency for certain crystals to respond best to balancing a particular ailment. But there are a number of books on this subject already, and in this book we are covering a much wider field of self-development. So we will just consider crystals on the way, as it were, and not as a subject of lifetime study in itself.

This planet Earth on which we live and move and have our being came into existence as the Universe began to solidify into the separate heavenly bodies. We've talked about the first primordial soup. When solid matter began to come into existence, it was preceded by hydrogen which, as the atoms combined together, made helium, a gas. Now helium makes light and its quite interesting that in the Bible, in Genesis, we have this description of the Lord making the world in seven days and 'there was darkness upon the face of the waters, and God said let there be light and there was light.' So somewhere in the myths and legends which give us symbolical and mystical ideas of the nature of the Universe and God and life itself, there is often some scientific truth.

There was light and it was caused by the gaseous element that stimulates the sense of sight -- helium. Though there is other light which we can't see with our eyes, those two little holes in the centre of our faces out of which we look at things. How strange it is that we see so much when we only have those two little apertures to look out of. But there is also light such as infra red light and ultra violet light which we can't actually make use of at all with our own eyes.

Its interesting that if crystals are shown under infra red light, one sees only darkness and then the crystals themselves come up in a myriad of different colours other than those that we see under ordinary light, as though light is shining out of themselves and all around is darkness. The vibrations of light which cannot be picked up by our eyes at all are at the extreme ends of the spectrum, the infra red and the ultra violet. Then there's the range of light and colour that we can ourselves see from semi-darkness right through to the brightness of a sunny day. It is interesting that moonlight conveys no colour at all. Even on the brightest moonlight night, when we can see quite a long way, everything is like a black and white photograph.

The Living Skin

This earth consists largely of the mineral kingdom: that is the various stages of solid matter, from the fires in the centre of the Earth, through many layers of solid matter up to near the surface where we have the 'crystal kingdom' where crystals and jewels are found; and then out on the surface where we ourselves live. Teilhard De Chardin who was a Roman Catholic priest and had many interesting philosophical and mystical ideas, described this earth as having a soft green outer skin. He said Gaia, the earth mother, is covered with a soft outer skin.

De Chardin was a remarkable man and had such deep understanding and such extraordinary ideas that Rome could not approve of him. So he was banished by his own Church, out into the Far East where he was required to live out his whole working life in a small community where there was nothing intellectually interesting for him to do and no outlet for his thoughts. He was intensely loyal to the Church. But all the time he was writing away, his deep mystical ideas, knowing that eventually they would be needed and made public. He had many contributions to make to the scientific as well as the mystical thought of this age.

He saw and described how everything on the surface of the Earth appears to stretch out towards the Sun. The soft outer skin consists of the great forests, all the grasslands, all vegetation and even the seas. In the old days it would have been much greener than it is now because we have caused so much damage on the surface of the earth with our sprawling cities and our cutting down of the rain forests and so on. But in fact Gaia, undamaged, has a green skin and all forms of organic life live either just under or on this surface, stretching up in the way that all trees and plants appear to stretch up towards the light.

We ourselves walking on two legs stretch up. Even animals walking on their four legs stretch up and out. If you could see the World spinning in space it would seem as though everything on it, even the little grasses, are all stretching out towards the Sun. Everything on the surface yearns towards the heat and light of the Sun, stretching out, needing the air to breathe and needing to receive water in the form of rain as it descends on this earth, while walking on the earth itself, which sustains it. Almost all forms of life feed either on each other or on the vegetation that grows on Gaia, Mother Earth, or on the minerals within.

Crystals grow not very far below the surface of the earth. They are hard and beautiful and very compressed. By tradition the king's crown was always adorned with jewels to represent the halo of the holy man, and crystals and particularly precious stones were thought of as having magical powers.

The principal jewels, of course, are the *diamond* which is colourless, simply reflecting the light; the *sapphire* a beautiful blue; the *emerald* a lovely green; *ruby* which is red. There is a variety of others. But the particularly precious stones are the ones which have always been revered and used by people either to decorate themselves, the king or the head man, or in some way used to represent something higher than man. Not only because they're beautiful but because it seems as though intuitively, even early men, knew there was something rather special about them.

They are a perfectly developed form of matter and their importance is deeply related to the energy which comes from the first cause. And with the first cause, with God, comes also the outflowing of the Spirit. So in a sense one can say that crystals reflect or even are an aspect of the Spirit. No wonder people revere and worship them.

All organic life takes in energy from the Sun and goes through a cycle of birth, development, maturity, procreation shrinking away and dying. All living organisms, whether in the form of vegetation or little free-living creatures or the primates or man himself, all form part of life on the surface of the earth: that is, organic life.

But the crystals below the surface of the earth are of the almost inert mineral realm. They have no cycle of events in their lives. They simply take in and give out energy in a perfectly balanced way. They just exist. They are perfection in its densest form and it is because they are so perfect that it has always been felt that they must in some way be extraordinary -- not only because they are beautiful to look at but because they have a strange feel to them. Therefore they are used both for exoteric matters, (that is for practical service in the world) and also in esoteric ways by those who understand the occult and the magical.

Their ability to balance is due to the unique arrangement of their atoms. The atom always tries to maintain balance. It consists of three main building blocks: proton, electron, neutron - positive, negative and neutral. We recognise positive, negative and neutral in electricity where we need to have the positive and negative in balance and earthed otherwise we get a great explosion. Three energy forms are needed to make balance and to make life. Both on the surface of the earth and within the earth itself the atomic realm holds good.

Free Energy

At the level of subatomic matter there is simply pure free energy which can pass through solid matter. Science now confirms what the mystics have always known. But at the level on the surface of the earth, the atom is directed and moved, not only by energy but by the existence of proteins, which come into being only above this basic crystal level - only on the green skin. All living things on the surface of the earth have proteins in them. In the crystal kingdom proteins are not found. Atoms in the mineral world are attracted and hold rigidly to each other forming a variety of unchanging patterns. The protein level is subject to continual change.

It's because of their unchanging patterns with their continual perfect atomic beat that we use crystals in quartz watches. The regular atomic beat is perfect for timekeeping. The old wind up watches used to have jewels in the back. I remember my grandfather showing me his fob watch when I was a child and all the jewels in the back, when the case was opened, and being told that makes it valuable. But, of course, the jewels were not there to make it valuable. They were there because they would make it a good timekeeper. The more the jewels, the more it kept perfect time. Now we use quartz in its own right without even the wind up mechanism because we understand it more.

Early wireless sets were crystal sets and they depended on the crystal to pick up sounds on the air waves. Crystals are used for many purposes where perfect timing is needed. They establish the speed of computers. Electronic chips are made with quartz for instance. So crystals are of great use in the ordinary material world. It's as though we've come from the perfection of the creator to a perfection at this fixed and final form of matter and we are learning to understand its possibilities. If God is energy and also Spirit we can perhaps experience God vibrating there in the crystals.

Nowadays most people think of crystals as useful tools for healing physical ailments. If you hold a crystal it can feel hot or cold; or heavier or lighter; or may seem to change as you hold it. It can seem to vibrate in your hand or to cause a tingling, something like an electric shock, right up your arm. The reason they can be used in healing appears to be the way they use their energy, taking in and giving out in like measure and also transforming energy into perfect balance.

Their colour is to do with the absorbency of certain wave lengths and is used very much in healing. Coloured lights or other coloured materials can also be used for healing of course. Colour can be said in a manner of speaking to be an impurity in the precious stones, or as a taking in of light at different wavelengths, instead of simply reflecting the pure light, as only the diamond does.

Colour is also associated with astrological ideas of the nature of the planets and the colours which are associated with those planets. The birth stones are also associated with the colours which are linked to the ruling planets. The idea of colour runs throughout a great deal of esoteric thought and we shall return to this later.

Although many people think of crystals mainly as a means of healing they are limited and need to be understood if they are to be used properly and effectively. It's almost as though the elemental energy running through the crystals could be thought of as directed by a higher will. But we need to remember that the crystal has no free will of its own. It has no duty. It just exists and all it has to do is just 'be', taking in and giving out energy in continual perfect balance. The crystal can't function or bring harmony at a higher level than itself except through the influence of a higher will. We may use a crystal with our own will and intention and in doing that we are trying to direct the elemental energy to aid us in our own creativity.

It's important not to get hooked on the idea of crystals as healers and to start putting ourselves under their authority. It's very important that they should be, if used at all, directed and under our authority. We on the surface of the earth are of a different level than the mineral kingdom beneath our feet. If we are going to use them we need to direct them and not let them direct us. But we do need to use them with respect, though not exactly with reverence except in the sense that there should be reverence for all forms of life.

Once when I was with Ra Bonewitz the American geologist, on a course on a farm in Oxfordshire, we were handling assorted crystals. He remarked 'I think these little creatures may be more finely attuned to God than we are.' He held them with the greatest respect. But never as though they were gods in themselves.

Working with Crystals

To continue with the idea in the last chapter, it would be good at this point to think of testing the reality of my statements on crystals by having a go, trying to 'do it yourself.' If possible, visit a crystal shop or healing fair or festival where there is a crystal stall, and have a really good look at what is on display. Buy one or two pieces - you will find that they are available from 50p or so up to several hundred pounds. It is important to handle any that you think of buying and see whether they feel right. Sometimes a crystal looks pleasing but seems as though it might not be on your own wavelength, when you have it in your hand. Sellers of crystals always expect you to want to touch and pick up, so don't be afraid to ask to do so.

There are a number of favourite crystals, and you will soon recognise some of them. The cloudy but colourless quartz, the deep mauve amethyst and the 'sticky toffee' gold citrine, for instance. These three always form hexagonal, that is six-sided peaks. Other types of crystals form natural cubes, or tetragons, or rhomboids, or derivatives of these.

Crystals are often cut and shaped. So distinguish, by looking, between the natural and man made shape. You will find that many of them are beautiful to look at and equally pleasing to the touch. You will also find among them, rose quartz and others which are not true crystals, but are crystalline. Rose quartz is usually offered in small lumps, or it may have been tumbled and polished to a smooth finish, like other crystalline stones. A tumbled stone is rather nice to have in your pocket, and finger in times of stress.

There are a number of basic families of crystals. All of them are like minor relations of the precious stones and jewels, which are usually far too expensive to buy: though if you have a ring with a diamond, sapphire, emerald or ruby, you may look at it with greater interest after examining its friends and relations! If you can never get to a crystal shop, even an attractive stone or pebble picked up on a beach or in your garden has some interesting qualities. Look for the sparkle of quartz in anything you find.

If you want to use a crystal for healing, this is what you should do. First of all think in terms of cleansing any crystal that you acquire. Perhaps you will buy one in a crystal shop or at a healing fair or somewhere, and you will know that your crystal will have been handled by other people before yourself. By tradition it should be washed in 'pure spring water'. But nowadays, we generally have to wash it under a cold running tap, because a fresh, running spring is not likely to be available. Let the tap run well until it is really clean, rinse the crystal, and then set it somewhere in the sun if possible for it to dry naturally. Don't leave it too long sitting in the sun because crystals belong under the earth in the dark and they're happier functioning in the dark than in the light. When it has dried itself then sit quietly with it, in a quiet room, and ponder on it, thinking in terms of what it looks like and what it might do and of its own innate perfect form and nature. God in the densest form of matter.

There is a tradition associated with crystal healing which says that you can programme a crystal with your thought. You may believe that this is so. It is not really provable but you can try. Perhaps the crystal you are using might have been programmed by someone else for some other purpose; so first of all, meditate upon it that it be clean and empty, free of other people's thoughts or any contamination that it might have. Then begin to programme it with your own quiet deep thoughts for whatever purpose you have in mind. Your direction should be something like 'that you be used to ease my mother's arthritis' for instance or 'for my sister's state of stress because of her broken marriage' or perhaps for some ailment of your own.

A Dense form of energy: Quartz Crystal

Quietly meditate while looking at your crystal, programming it in this way and then, when you have finished, take your crystal to your mother or whoever it may be wanting the crystal and put it on a shelf or mantelpiece or by the bed or wherever suitable, drawing attention to it. Its quiet steady vibration may indeed ease the troubled person. Many people say that they get considerable benefit, feel calmer and better generally, their spirits lift, if they hold a crystal or have one sitting near them and consider and contemplate it. It is undoubtedly of value because of its balancing abilities; not because it can bring new energy in itself but because it can balance the energy in you and make you feel better.

Now I must give you a warning against too much credulity! We don't know whether we really can programme crystals by thought. It's a matter of opinion whether we can, but we might be able to. So think in terms of, they must serve us and we can use them, with courtesy and respect. But they must not use us. This applies to all the four elemental kingdoms -- we are higher than all the elemental kingdoms, and we shall discuss this further in the next chapter. They must not use us; but we must be aware of them, and I think courtesy is required towards all forms of life on this earth because they are all God in the form of matter.

Don't Get Hooked!

Many of the old fairy tales and myths and legends, particularly of Ireland and the western Isles of Scotland, speak of 'the little folk'. They experience a mixture of pleasure and fear of the little folk. We have all read legends of how the gnomes will come and help people in the night, will harvest the field which could not be harvested because the old man is ill; or they will replace something which is lost, or in some way make people's lives easier. But they say the little folk have to be placated, so people would put bread and milk outside their doors for the gnomes or elves or fairies to take at night.

In the old days there was a mixture of reverence and terror towards the little folk. It does seem that the idea of these little creatures of the creator with their power and their possible ability to turn nasty, is in some way connected with the existence of the mineral kingdom and its possible use and possible power over us. They seem to be of the earth element. Therefore be alert and awake to what you are doing with crystals. A crystal will tend to draw you inwards and downwards because it comes from inside the earth. It may be that we think that we need to go upwards and outwards towards the godhead. But both are needed. God above is the perfect One. Coming down into matter He becomes multiplicity. God in the crystal form is also One. Here is complete balance, and coming upwards into the light He seems to go into multiplicity again.

When people get hooked on crystals and almost worship them, they gradually turn in more and more within themselves and ultimately are obeying inner voices which are below the level of mankind. They are not fulfilling mankind's possibilities and purposes on this earth. The purpose of mankind must be higher than that of the mineral kingdom. We should treat the crystals with courtesy and respect but never be at their mercy. They cannot be conscious in the way that we are growing in consciousness. Their consciousness can only ever be at the level of the elemental kingdom. They exist through aeons of time, growing a little and always remaining the same in their essence. But we, mankind, are destined to move on.

Try considering the difference between the crystal kingdom and the life forms on the surface of the earth. If you hold something like a horse chestnut or acorn or a seed pod in one hand and a crystal in the other, you may see with great clarity the difference between the two kingdoms. The crystal vibrating there quietly will never do anything but just exist. It has no will of its own, no duty, no inner impulse other than just to be.

A 'conker' is an extraordinary thing. If you manage to pick it off a tree or find one on the ground under the tree, in its big green rather prickly shell, and break it open, you know how within the shell you find a wonderful shiny mahogany horse chestnut. It has been cradled in a kind of white velvety womb which has protected it until it is ready to come out into the air. It holds within it the enormous potential of a living, growing, developing being of the organic/protein level of creation. You can almost feel a different type of life vibrating in it, which can push a little sprout up into the light and a root down into the soil. If you planted it in the ground in Autumn, by the Spring it might have put out little roots pushing down into the earth, which it needs to sustain it. The shell will break open, and small shoots push up onto the surface, into the air, into the sunlight and the rain which it requires to feed it. It requires the elemental kingdom to support it. In a couple of years it can push out a few leaves, a slightly more woody stem and ultimately it becomes a tree with long tendril flowers which are white or pink and with a slight scent to them. As it gets bigger, over the years, it will start to produce seed pods, the big green spiky seed pods which hold further conkers, shiny mahogany coloured seeds which can make other trees.

Over many years, that thing that you are holding in your hand at the moment, so small and compact, can become a tree much bigger than you are. It can live for hundreds of years pushing out its own flowers, its own seed pods, its own conkers falling to the ground for squirrels to eat or carry away, or little boys to play with. Unimpeded, more trees will grow and as the parent tree becomes old and frail and begins to shrink and rot away into the ground, it becomes food for the earth. The younger trees will be getting big and strong and in their own right re-creating the parent tree in a new generation. Cycles and cycles over aeons of time of trees, great forests of trees which could come from that one thing you are holding in your hand. Ponder on this strange phenomenon.

It is said that by the time we are five years old wonderment and amazement at life has already begun to go as we take things for granted! If we could recreate in ourselves the wonder of early childhood, we can see how extraordinary it is that such a small object as a seed has within it the genetic knowledge to make an enormous tree and to go on repeating the cycles of birth, development, procreation, shrinking and dying -- the phenomenon of organic life continuing on this earth, changing through the generations to some extent but always looking after itself as though with a will and intention of its own. A will and intention beyond the will and intention of the crystal kingdom.

If you garden, you will have discovered that the will and intention of a plant can be quite strong; if you try to make it go a way it does not want to go it will go back. If you wind it clockwise around a support or stake and it wants to go anticlockwise it will unwind itself and get itself back into its natural way of growing. Some climbing plants always go clockwise and other species always anticlockwise. Some plants will spread more than you want them to and others will hardly grow at all. It appears that they are directed by a will of their own or by some will beyond what can direct the mineral kingdom. These things, so simple and elementary that even a child knows them, are often overlooked by the adult mind which takes them all so much for granted. It is worth considering anew the extraordinary nature of life at the plant level, and the even more extraordinary life of the higher organisms which move freely on the surface of the earth.

Mankind surely has a higher possibility still, in that we can observe all this and, to some extent direct or perhaps impede, help or destroy, all these things which we take so much for granted. We could be sufficiently awake and conscious to want to work positively with them instead of trying to subdue nature. This does seem rather important. Of course we can use for good and legitimate purposes all the good creatures of the creator that we know about. Yet above us there are possibly those who can use and direct us ourselves, for higher purposes. We might be able to serve in higher kingdoms, in the way the crystals serve us. We need to ponder all these things and understand them in our own way.

Suggested Exercises.

1. Get a piece of crystal, or even a crystallised stone from the beach or from the garden. Then find a seed pod, a berry or flower. Meditate on their nature as you hold them one in each hand. Really look at them and feel deeply what they are like, what their possibilities are.

2. Buy one or two pieces of crystal and experiment as described in the previous pages. Wash, cleanse and programme them, for calming and healing purposes. You will almost certainly experience something. Make your own judgement.

3

Elements and Elementals

Our bodies are made entirely from the elements which are available to us on this earth: the air which we can breathe without suffocating and the food that we need to sustain our bodies, the water and the heat of the sun. But there is obviously something in life beyond the elements. Perhaps the spirit? Perhaps intelligence? If the first cause is energy then clearly something is carried on that energy. Intelligence seems to exist at all levels of life. So perhaps it is just intelligence. Our intelligence is clearly higher than that of the animals, but there must be other intelligences way above our level, for we ourselves could not have made the world! Perhaps a great mind of enormous intelligence is behind the whole phenomenon of life. So we must develop our intelligence if we want to grow in consciousness -- the consciousness of what we are and what the world may be.

Intelligence can be perceived at all levels, but it can only be perceived as it manifests via the elements: e.g. by what visible actions can be seen to result, what the body can be seen to be doing, etc. So let's define the elements more precisely. In the west we think of four elements; earth, water, fire and air. But the oriental teachings have a fifth element which is sometimes defined as space or as ether. It appears as though the elements manifest themselves in or through the fifth element.

Our flesh, our bones and sinews, are made of the earth element and the minerals that are in the earth. We have trace elements of all minerals in our bodies. Our bodies are also largely made of water -- so the blood and the water within our bodies come from the second element. The third element, fire, is carried via the heart and the venous system; and of course the heat and warmth of the body is entirely due to the heat of the sun -- though it varies in its intensity and is sometimes withdrawn to comparative cold. But without the heat from the sun which we reflect and take in through our skin and our breathing, we could not maintain life at all. All organic life of all sorts breathes in and out and this is the air element.

All the elements are necessary to maintain life: but it's very interesting to look at the length of time that we can endure without each one of them. This has a lot of significance. We can endure many days or possibly even weeks without an intake of solid food, (that is, without the earth element,) providing we have water. The body however can only endure for a matter of days if it has no solid food and no water. If it has no solid food and no water and no heat whatsoever (for instance if a man is shut in a refrigerator) then it can endure only a matter of hours. Without any heat at all the temperature within the body will sink so low that the body will freeze solid and in a matter of hours the heart will stop. Without air the body can exist for only a matter of minutes. After a couple of minutes suffocation starts, the brain cells begin to die and the whole body then dies. So it is interesting to see that the level of existence without the elements is much longer without the solid or heavier elements and much shorter without the lighter elements. Obviously the vibrations of the heavier elements are much slower than those of the lighter ones such as fire and air. And then the fifth element of space or ether: we can never tell exactly what it is, but maybe we can't exist without that at all!

Possibly crystals may have their energy trapped entirely in solid matter, very slow long living solid matter. By comparison our life is short; we grow to maturity, procreate ourselves and then fade away and die because we are in the life cycle of, not minerals, but organic life. But that which we live in -- space? ether? -- may be very long-lived: tied to the life cycle of this planet, or perhaps eternal? We don't know, and we can ponder, on what that fifth element may actually be.

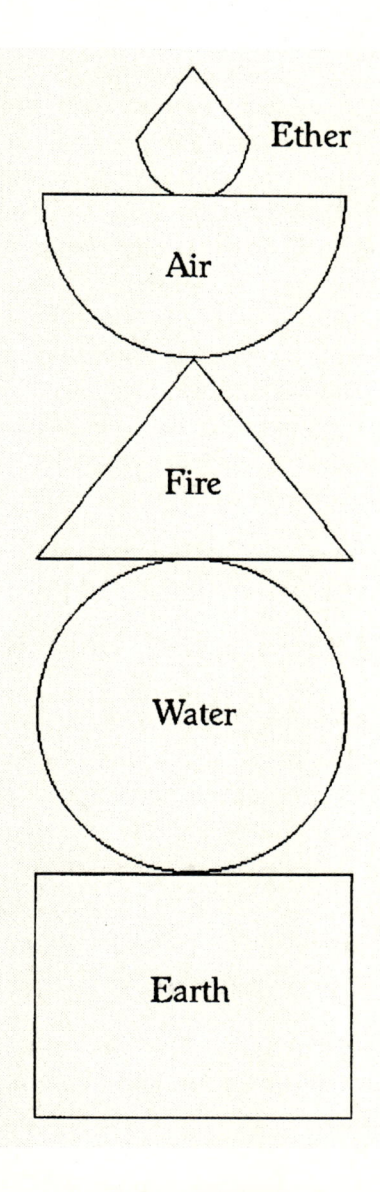

The Pagoda:
The elements shown in traditional temples

An understanding of the elements goes very far back in history. For instance, the pagodas and the temples of the orient are built to illustrate the idea of the four elements. Basically the temples and pagodas show themselves as being grounded in earth, They have a solid or square base which is associated with the idea of the earth element. On top of that base is a storey which is generally roughly circular and represents water. On top of that is something which is more or less triangular and representing fire and on top of that is something rather like an upturned saucer which represents the air element reaching upwards. And yet above that is a kind of onion-shaped dome representing ether, or the fifth element, which reaches higher still outside our realm of knowledge or understanding.

The Physical Vehicle

The same order of elements is seen by tradition in the body. Many old diagrams show this. According to esoteric tradition, the earth element is associated with the feet and legs, which walk on the earth. The water element with the digestive system, kidneys, liver, bladder etc. The fire element with the heart and the arterial system. The air element with the head, the mouth and nose which breathe in and out. Ether, or the fifth element under any other name, is above and around the body.

The elements are seen also in many other esoteric traditions such as palmistry or handreading, or the Chinese discipline known as cheirology -- studying a person's nature and tendencies by studying the hand. An earth hand for instance has a rather square palm and short fingers. By tradition the mind set which goes with an earth hand, is the phrase 'I will endure'. A water hand has a long palm and long fingers -- a more delicate and subtle hand than the earth hand which is rooted in common sense. The water hand goes with the mind set 'How do I feel?' The fire hand has a long palm and relatively short fingers. The mind set for the fiery hand is the urgent 'When can I do it?' The impatience of fire! The air hand has a large square palm and long fingers. The mind set for the air element, which is intellectual on the whole, is 'What does it mean?'

Very few people have a hand which shows purely one element or another. Apart from hand shaping, the elements are manifested in many other ways, such as the texture of the skin and the markings on the palm, the fingers and the general look of the hand itself. But broadly by ancient traditions they give a type linked more to one element than to another. The down to earth type, the sensitive watery type, the fiery impatient type and the intellectual thought-filled air type.

Astrology also links human kind very much to the elements and a horoscope chart shows whether a person is mainly earthy, watery, fiery or airy according to the strength of the planets within the signs of the Zodiac. The signs being broadly speaking: the earth signs are Capricorn, Taurus and Virgo; the water signs are Pisces, Cancer and Scorpio; the fire signs are Aries, Leo and Sagittarius; the air signs of Aquarius, Gemini and Libra. All the signs of the Zodiac are muted and qualified by many other indications so that, just as with hand readings, in astrology almost nobody is entirely made of one element.

All the same, the fact that the elements are so much linked with the old methods of knowing ourselves and finding ourselves is very interesting. It suggests that our bodies and minds are much linked, and undoubtedly the bodies are largely elemental but the minds possibly reach out towards the fifth element. In cheirology, it is the thumb which is associated with ether, whereas the fingers are linked with the four elements recognised in the West. The little finger is the air finger, the next or ring finger is the fire finger, the next is the earth finger and the finger next to the thumb is the water finger. The thumb, connected with ether, is the way into finer realms.

The studies of Cheirology or hand reading, Astrology, the

Chakras or psychic centres of the body, or The Tree of Life are all part of the subjects which we ought to touch on in this book. We will not spend ages on any of them but will simply define them in the context of whatever we are dealing with at any one point in the book.

The World of the Fairies

The elements are clearly the vehicles for the life force. But they are not the life force themselves. We don't know what the life force is; we don't know what is Spirit, though most people would acknowledge that the spirit does exist. We need to think about and understand in our own way what the spirit may be. We need to consider our own body and this definition of spirit and body. Does it seem to have reality? Is the body You or is it simply the vehicle with which you travel through this world? And what else is there?

Because we have intelligence and imagination, mankind has made up many stories, myths and legends. All cultures have fairy tales. Fairy tales suggest the existence of beings who are made up of, or represent, the elements and are said to be the spirits of the elements. It's quite interesting to consider these.

Paracelsus was a Fifteenth Century Swiss physician and alchemist. His real name was Theophrastus Bombastus von Hohenheim. This is where the word 'bombastic' comes from. So he must have been a bit inclined to hold forth! But he had ideas, and they have lasted to this day. He gave names to his own ideas of the nature spirits which he could conceive: gnomes, elves, undines, salamanders and sylphs. The gnomes were said to be dwarfish spirits of a subterranean race who guarded earth's treasures: e.g the mineral realm of the crystals. Elves were mischievous spirits who lived on the surface of the earth. They sat on or lived under toadstools, and are often depicted that way in fairy tales. This of course is quite curious as it links to the whole 'magic mushroom' phenomena! As we know in this day and age, hallucinations and visions can come from eating certain toadstools known as magic mushrooms. The gnomes and the elves were of the earth element, associated entirely with the earth and the gnomes were generally dressed in brown and the elves in green with pointed hats. They were male.

Associated with the water element were the undines, who were flowing creatures rarely pictured except in a water form. They were female. Associated with the fire element was the salamander. This is a real lizard type creature which was thought by Paracelsus to live in the fire. He defined them as male. And the sylphs were of the air element and always had wings. They were a type of fairy and obviously female.

There are earlier legends, before Paracelsus, that speak of nature spirits and indicate that nature may manifest itself in the form of the elements. The Elementals are the spirits within those elements.

In a slightly different category are nymphs, who are also female elemental spirits, but who yearn to serve a higher deity. They gave rise to the term nympholepsy, which means a frenzy of desire for the unattainable. And also, of course, nymphomania, which means a frenzy or ecstasy of sexual desire. These mythological beings are not content with their lot, like the nature spirits, but yearn towards something else. So they have some common aspirations with mankind.

Another category is the idea of the divas, which are traditionally master spirits ruling a certain place. The diva of the lake, or garden etc., has given rise to the word Diva meaning a master musician etc. The Hindu word dev or Deva, meaning holy or godlike, is obviously related.

There are many fairy tales which describe the spirits as being able to look after or serve mankind or to help us. Nearly always they carry a kind of sting in the tail in the sense that the elemental spirits can turn against man if man refuses to continue to serve them. So the warning that they should serve us and we should not serve them, comes in many fairy tales.

Apart from fairy tales for children, the tales told around the peat fires in Scotland and Ireland, speak of a really strong belief in fairies as a possible actual level of existence. People will still avoid inconveniencing the fairies, and apologise to them if they think they might be annoyed. At one time I was often in the Isle of Skye in the Hebrides. I remember a farmer who accidentally damaged a 'fairy dun'-- a prehistoric pit dwelling on his land. He was convinced the fairies lived in the duns. He took an offering out at night and put it where his plough had caused the damage, and made his courteous apologies. 'I wouldna want tae hurt them,' he said.

History records the phenomenon of the Cottingley fairies. These were apparent fairies photographed with a Brownie camera, in 1917. at the time of Sir Arthur Conan Doyle. Conan Doyle is better known of course as being the author and inventor of the Sherlock Holmes stories. But he was also an occultist, or dabbler in the paranormal. He came across the Cottingley fairy photographs and investigated very thoroughly what they might be.

These photographs are extraordinarily convincing, I have seen the original prints at Tekels Park (a property near London belonging to the Theosophical Society) where they are pinned up on a wall of a summer house. They are all in brown sepia print and are curling at the corners and look extraordinarily realistic pictures of fairies moving about in trees and bushes and among the flowers. They were photographed by Elsie Wright, aged 15, and her 10 year old cousin Frances Griffiths. They declared repeatedly over many years that they really had seen fairies and photographed them.

When Conan Doyle became interested in them, he did his utmost to test the reality of whether the fairies existed. The children said that they did exist, but that they could not show them to the adults because no adults would be able to see them and the fairies wouldn't like it if the adults went into the woods with them. Conan Doyle provided a new film for the Brownie camera, and had also had the camera itself tested to make sure that it was a perfectly ordinary camera. The children went back to the woods and returned with more photographs. The films were tested afterwards under laboratory conditions and could not be faulted. They seemed to be perfectly genuine photographs of perfectly genuine spirits like fairies.

Of course many people did not believe they were genuine. Conan Doyle, who was an intelligent man, had many doubts but he tested again and again and questioned the children until such a time as he became convinced that they were genuine photographs of fairies.

Over many years as they grew up the children continually, when questioned, declared that they were genuine and that they did really see the fairies and could photograph them. But in later years, while the younger girl refused to speak at all, the older girl said on one occasion that they were not real and that they had made them themselves out of paper. And then she said no more. So she appeared to have blown the story! However, the fairies in the pictures are so clear -- many of those early Victorian pictures were extraordinarily clear and almost better than the photos we take today-- and they look so genuine that it's very difficult to believe that two little girls could possibly have made them out of paper. So it's tempting to think that the girl was so tired of being questioned and disbelieved over the years that to get rid of the questioners she simply said that they had made them. But that they were, in fact, genuine all the time. What can we possibly believe of this phenomenon of the Cottingley fairies? Were they real? Could imagination somehow bring such things into being? Are there really fairies at the bottom of the garden? Many people believe that they have seen fairies, but many don't want to admit it unless they are thought completely crack pot!

Psychic Imagination

The idea of discarnate intelligence's and the angelic kingdom could possibly be said to belong to the whole realm of man's imagination or insight or intuition or psychic ability. The psyche is clearly higher than ordinary intelligence but does not seem to be the same as the Spirit. Maybe the psyche is the soul.

My brother-in-law Rodney Collin, the philosopher, once wrote 'the soul can be wedded to the desires of the body or the aspirations of the spirit'. If one thinks of the psyche in that sense, it could be said that the attention could be turned either to the elemental kingdoms and all their fascination and possibilities or to the angelic kingdom and ideas of the godhead and the eternal and unchanging presence of almighty God Himself: the First Cause.

Because we are in the world and must be of the world, it's perfectly right to be aware of all these things both above and below ourselves, and it can be helpful to understand our own nature and look at all these things and perhaps allow our imagination to have full play to the extent of considering whether we believe in fairies. Of course, if you believe in fairies you may never see one but if you don't believe in fairies it is quite certain that you will never see one!

Intelligence appears to exist at all levels, and for all we know it may exist in a strange almost unchanging way within the crystal kingdom itself. It certainly exists at all levels of organic life as we know it. Even plants have a simple intelligence. They know to close their petals against the cold and the dark and open to the sun in the morning. They know to stay dormant under the ice of the frozen ground in Winter and to push strongly upwards towards the sun in the warming days of Spring. One might say it is instinct or unconscious force which makes these things happen, but I think it is reasonable to call it a type of intelligence.

I remember an old gardener once looking at all the daisies

coming up rapidly all over the close cut lawn, very soon after he had mown it, and saying 'Canny little things daisies! They looks round and they says to themselves, 'better not come up on a long stalk here. We shall get cut down'. Daisies do of course come up on long stalks in the hedgerows and in the fields which are not cut so frequently. But on a lawn, if you look at them, when the lawn is cut weekly or so, they have very short stalks and flower very close to the ground, as if they know they have to flower and spread their seed to procreate themselves in their short life span. Somehow they know this and they struggle to achieve it. This is a kind of intelligence. They seek a means to achieve their own purpose.

Animals, even simple animals, know how to look for food, to find shelter in Winter, to nurture and protect their young. Domestic animals, living with us, learn much more. The dog who goes to the door waiting for his owner before the owner can be seen or even heard, is using his instinct and his intelligence. The instinct says his master is coming and the intelligence causes him to get up and go to the door because he knows his master will come through that front door. Many animals certainly have a sense which we haven't got or we have lost. It manifests via the intelligence. Perhaps it is psychic imagination.

Some animals do very complex reasoning; like squirrels who will struggle to find how to get nuts out of a bird nut container for instance. Even if it's made very difficult and complex they will struggle and find a way to get hold of the nuts intended for the birds. Some animals will use tools of one sort or another to suck up termites for instance for food, or to make a bed. And it must be intelligence that weaves a complex bird's nest. The instinct tells the bird to make the nest in order to lay the eggs and sit on them but it must be intelligence that causes the complex weaving in and out of the stalks. Some birds' nests are very beautiful. In the same way the spider's web, although made by instinct in a manner of speaking, is also very beautiful and must have a kind of intelligence behind it. If you look at a cobweb covered with dew on an Autumn morning, you will know how lovely and how perfect it can be.

So intelligence is not the same as imagination but there is a strong connection between the two. First the animal must by imagination realise that a home or a nest is needed, or that the young are hungry and food must be found and brought to them. Instinct or imagination maybe. The imagination aids them and the intelligence causes them to go out and find food or whatever is needed.

In the same way, imagination aids us to get what we want. At the level of mankind, everything we make or do, or invent for our own well-being starts in the realm of the imagination. If you are hungry you visualise a meal and your tongue can almost taste it, your mouth will water in anticipation of eating. You visualise the food you want, you make the meal or you go and buy it having decided what you want. The menu in a restaurant is experienced by imagination via your memory. You can taste the food, meat or fish or vegetarian, sweet and sour in your imagination. The intelligence selects and chooses and your imagination tells you what you will get when you have chosen. If you had no imagination you wouldn't be able to know what was coming at all when the plate was put down in front of you.

We live by our imagination far more than we realise. By using our imagination we can recreate the faces of friends from our past, loved faces from long ago or colleagues and associates today. You can say to yourself: I'll be in my mother's house, or somewhere else, and the eyes of your imagination will present you with a picture of what was once known or is known today. Even by efforts of recall you can see rooms from long ago, furniture or pictures almost forgotten and bring them back into reality again. It's worth trying this to see what you can bring out.

Imagination as a Tool

Ideas of things that you'd like to carry out can also go through the programme of your imagination. If you would like to climb a mountain you can imagine climbing, the gear on your body, the heavy boots, ropes, tackle, the exertion of having to breathe finer air. Even if you've never been on a mountain, because you've seen pictures and films you can create in your mind the feeling of it. Imagination is an extraordinary function of the human mind, a great tool.

The Maharishi Mahesh Yogi used to say to his people that you can get what you want with your imagination. He used to say if you want a Cadillac, say to yourself every day 'I am the owner of a Cadillac' and one day you will own one! We used to laugh, partly because we didn't particularly want a Cadillac and partly because we didn't believe it any way. But maybe this is the meaning of the saying in the Bible 'with faith you can move mountains'. Who knows whether with faith or imagination, whatever that might be, it might not be possible to get whatever we want. For instance, could imagination have created the Cottingley fairies?

After all, the first man who thought of inventing a machine to do his sums for him was in a manner of speaking the creator of the whole computer system. His imagination caused him to think 'I could make a machine which will do the donkey work for me'. An astronomer called John Couch Adams, the director of the observatory at Cambridge, who discovered the planet Neptune made one of the first mathematical calculators. When he was still an undergraduate, he was trying to pinpoint the exact position of the planet Neptune, whose existence he suspected as a result of what is known as the 'inverse perturbations' of Uranus. He spent many hours, days, weeks and months doing very complex calculations. One day, sitting in his study in St. John's College, Cambridge and doing his sums as usual in the early hours of the morning (he used to work through the night sometimes), he thought it was very boring and it should be possible to invent something to avoid all this. He invented the first calculator which could add up, subtract, multiply and divide. It was large and cumbersome. But it did the job. So by his imagination he was one of the originators of the whole world of mathematical calculators and the whole computerised kingdom of today -- because other people's imagination and intelligence took up his idea and developed it further and further.

The squirrel, which in a mixture of imagination, hunches and intelligence, collects nuts and buries them for the Winter and then makes his dray to lie warm and snug, is a simpler creature than we are. But all living things have their imagination and can use their consciousness to some extent. So with our imagination and our intelligence we can begin to grow. We are higher than the squirrels and the whole animal kingdom. We might be able to bring great things into being for the future of this rather perilous world if we think positively, if we think creatively and use our imagination.

If we work via the body, this elemental body, our possibilities are enormous. If we use all the five senses which are experienced via the elements -- sight, hearing, taste, touch and smell -- if we use all those attributes and we use all our body's experience and our mind's experience and our imagination then we create ideas. So the elements are basic but all those finer attributes of the intelligence and if the imagination, can lead us into the fields of creativity; into the creative line via the psyche, and perhaps ultimately to the Spirit or the godhead itself.

Suggested Exercises

1. In imagination, conjure up the faces of friends, places and people that have disappeared into the past.

2. In imagination, conjure up something you would like to do or to have. Try to start to bring it into being by this means.

3. Get a book of classic children's fairy tales, such as Langs Fairy Tales. Reread them considering whether you think they portray a kingdom lower than our own. Do they suggest beings who might help us, or who with us might nurture and help to develop this planet earth? But is there a warning inherent in them? What is the nature of the warning?

There's a difference between simple fairy tales and the great myths and legends of mankind which deal with archetypal forces. We will consider these later for they speak of the levels of the angels and of gods.

4

If Gaia is Mother, who is Father?

In my small spinney, up at the top of a winding woodland path and steps at my country cottage in Norfolk, a great drift of bluebells is graced by the Spring sunlight beneath the trees. Because I am in my eighties, I climb the steps slowly, trace the short path between the sycamore trees, the silver birches, the holly and the hazel, and reach the oak bench and chairs which stand at the viewpoint. From here I can look down on my semi-wild garden, and across fields and farmland to the distant skyline. Looking about me at the lush young growth and smelling the warm, 'green scents' it is easy to feel the living, breathing presence of Gaia, the earth mother, with all her fecundity and profusion of gifts. But if Gaia is Mother, who or what, I ask myself, is Father?

According to custom and tradition, Mother nurtures and Father tends to discipline the growing child. But if we think in terms of Gaia, Mother Earth with her fertility and riches maintaining all forms of life and providing the means for us to live and exist in this world, what place is there for a Father at all?

The American Indians speak of Mother Earth and Father Sky: and there are plenty of old traditions and ideas which suggest that the feminine element is that which is below our feet and that the masculine principle manifests itself 'up there' and outside in some way. That's all a bit airy fairy so let's think what Gaia and the parental principles may actually be.

Nobody likes to think nowadays of the word discipline. It sounds too much like smacking children and that sort of thing. It's almost politically incorrect! But in fact the word discipline comes from the Latin word *discere* which is simply 'to learn'. The word disciple also comes from it, and also discern. So to learn from someone who knows rather more, and to accept the need to listen to that person is really the whole meaning of the word discipline.

Of course no one wants a master figure nowadays, especially in these days when the feminine element is so very dominant. But all the same, everybody recognises that young children and other young creatures have to be taught in some way. They can't teach themselves very much. The mother role is essentially that of protecting and caring for the young when they are too immature to know what to do or even how to look after themselves in the simplest way: to feed, to protect, to take care of and to give elemental understanding of the world around them. But the role of the male principle appears to be that of teaching and providing the knowledge that is necessary for the growing child to realise his own potential and to know how to make a life for himself in this world. In the same way, the winds and the rain, the heat and the cold, by turns seem to 'discipline' the trees and the flowers, which learn to withstand adversity and flourish under continually changing circumstances.

In the past, the paternal role as teacher tended to be stern and 'disciplinarian' in its harshest sense. Children sitting in rows in school where often cowed into obedience by the ever present threat of punishment. But the intention was the laudable one of encouraging them to listen to and learn the 'disciplines' -- such as the discipline of mathematics, of science, of the arts and so on.

In fact, of course, what children need is to be taught how to exercise self discipline. Without willing attention to the teaching which is available, their adventurousness or natural indolence can get them into all sorts of trouble and scrapes as well as real danger in life. But whatever the educational system available, most children gradually learn codes of behaviour and ethical beliefs that will help them as they grow up and take responsibility for themselves. Of course, this is the theory of education! In practice it may not work so well. Education is more geared to practical and mundane matters nowadays. There is not much school teaching on the philosophical and spiritual side for young people of really enquiring minds who begin to ask the eternal question: Who am I? What is it all about?

There was once a great tradition which is known as Esoteric School or occult school. Traces of this way of teaching can be found very far back indeed in all parts of the world. It appears to have existed in ancient China in what used to be known as pre-cataclysmic times -- that is the period in which all the ancient occult teachings such as astrology, numerology, cheirology, iridology and the inexact or complete occult sciences began. A time before known history, before Noah's flood. Nobody knows how far back.

Tradition of Esoteric School

Apart from these shadowy beginnings, there are traces of esoteric type schools, or occult schools that can be much more easily examined and thought about. We have in society today the remnant of a number of ancient esoteric schools which have come down into ordinary every day usage but which stemmed originally from very profound sources. The Freemasons for instance claim their descent from the 'school' teaching of Solomon. This was deeply connected with the idea of the building of the great temple of Jerusalem. Jerusalem was thought to be the main power spot on the whole of the earth, and it's claimed by the three religions of revelation -- Judaism, Christianity and Islam. They all believe that it is their particular holy place. As a result they have tended to fight over it through all the generations.

Solomon it was who was supposed to have built the original holy temple. He seemed to have had some understanding of the energy rising from the earth in that holy spot, knowledge of what we may call these days geodetic lines. Dowsing was almost certainly used to find the area in which power rising from the earth's centre and reaching up to the heavens could be tapped. The whole temple would then have been built using the esoteric knowledge of number, of the value of exact measurements, according to tradition, to get a very powerful centre that would be suitable for study, learning and worship.

This was all, of course, long before the birth of Jesus Christ. But Freemasons, later on, seemed to have some inherited knowledge, alongside the Christian teaching which they espoused. They wandered throughout Europe and were particularly powerful in France where they were behind the building of the great Gothic cathedrals. And indeed even in this country, in England, many of the churches and cathedrals were built by Freemasons. They were almost the first trade union! Builders who would not be beholden to any master in their trade, so tending to be outside society. If you wanted to build a church, send for the Freemasons -- the wandering band of masons who knew more than other people how to make use of the land, of the earth and all the powers there, in such a way as to help attain the glories of the Spirit. Nowadays of course the Freemasons are almost no more than a gentleman's club, but they still have their initiation ceremonies and their secret signs which are deeply connected with the idea of masons who knew how to construct and how to build. They carried with them, and still have within their ranks, the idea of the discipline of learning, of service to others and to God, and of giving and of creating in some way.

In the same way the Knights Hospitallers and the Knights Templars were the remnants of esoteric schools. The Knights Hospitallers were first founded in the tenth century as were the Knights of St John of Jerusalem who installed themselves to protect the holy sepulchre against marauding herds and people who were impeding the devout travellers and pilgrims who wanted to go and worship at the sepulchre. They wore a plain black garment with a white cross upon it, a white cross with rather large arms. Most of us can think immediately where that uniform can still be seen today: the St John Ambulance brigade are those that followed on from the days of the Knight Hospitallers. In later years they were based in Malta and the square, wide-armed white cross still being worn today by the St John Ambulance Brigade is called the Maltese cross. Of course the profound knowledge of mathematics and of secret learning has been lost long ago. But there remains the idea of service to others and the idea of being very alert, very awake to the needs of a situation -- in fact to be conscious of what is going on and to have the know-how to respond to any emergency.

The Knights Templars were another great order, primarily a military one, but again with a lot of secret knowledge behind them. They were founded in the eleventh century and also protected the great temple of Jerusalem against those who also claimed it for their own. They were involved in the Crusades: Christian battles against the Muslims, whom they thought of as the Infidels, but who also clearly had some claim to Jerusalem. Effigies of crusaders in churches show them with crossed legs, the sign of an initiate. They wore a white garment with a red cross superimposed on it. We recognise that today as being the sign of the Red Cross. The Red Cross still does an enormous amount of work in times of war or famine or disaster, helping and aiding in any emergency and giving their kindness, their will, their knowledge and practical teaching assistance -- though probably not all the people who work with the Red Cross would realise that their body comes from a very ancient and interesting esoteric sect.

Knowledge from the ancient esoteric schools, with its frequently rather hard discipline and clear system of learning, became muted and modified through the years. It became the basis of ordinary society and changed into forms of purely worldly use. By tradition the ancient schools had initiation ceremonies. The young aspirant had to commit himself to the particular discipline he was entering, by undergoing ordeals of some kind, which might be either very difficult or very frightening. This was to test a novice's worth, to see whether he was really willing to be committed to learn and to fulfil himself through the discipline that he had decided to accept.

This was all very male orientated. The Eleusian Mysteries seemed to have put would-be initiates through fearful and life-threatening events. The legends told in Mallory's Le Morte d'Arthur show the young squire awaiting his knighthood, kneeling alone before the altar of an empty chapel all through the preceding night, holding his sword aloft -- a feat of considerable endurance. The initiation ceremonies of the Freemasons today of course, echo the old customs in a very simple way. And Army or school initiation of new recruits, now often debased into cruel or sadistic acts, are a corrupted form of what was originally intended by 'initiation.' The ordeal was meant to bring about some deliberate change of the attitude of a student or aspirant, and enable him to see the truth newly, test his own courage, and therefore take command of himself with a sense of growing purpose.

As Above, So Below

The occult sciences, which include ritual magic, alchemy, the tarot, astrology, numerology and so on, are a vast number of inexact or incomplete sciences which tend to be known in the esoteric tradition as 'rejected knowledge'. They're based on a system of correspondences (as above, so below) etc. They carry a magical viewpoint of life and the idea that individuals by study, effort, taking part in rituals, disciplines and other means, can acquire some kind of stature or even power for themselves. The reason society and the establishment rejects them is not only because they can't be understood or justified by reason, but also because they tend to give stature to the individual as opposed to the vested interest of the establishment. They were originally almost entirely a male preserve. The male role of knowledge and teaching and of intellectual debate contrasted with the feminine role of feeling, of nurturing and caring.

The true characteristics of magical belief is in the system of correspondences, Astrology is perhaps most fruitful of these manifestations 'As Above, So Below' is the most famous of the Hermetic maxims. The Hermetica is a vast collection of miscellaneous writings which, by tradition, stem from the god Hermes or Mercury or the Egyptian god Thoth which may mean truth. Thoth was said to be the originator of writing and all the arts; that is drawing in hieroglyphics or little pictures to convey knowledge. Hermes in mythology is the father of astrology, alchemy and all the magical rites and the revealer of all occult correspondences. The semi mythical Hermes Trismegistus, which means thrice great Hermes, carried on the tradition. Magistus of course comes from the word magus or magic -- the three wise men were the three magi of which magus is the singular. The root word is imagination, image and so on. And Hermes has come down to us as meaning sealed, closed or secret, hermetically sealed for instance.

The basic doctrine which springs from this occult tradition in the West, is the belief that it is possible to have a direct knowledge of God and of things Divine either from mystical experiences or by possession of secret doctrines which are handed down to initiates from pagan, Greek and Jewish Gnostic channels. This is the line that runs throughout the Hermetica. And the knowledge which is said to ensure the growth and development of mankind, is that each individual contains a spark of God and must awake from the half life or the dreams or the intoxication or the 'sleep' of life on earth to a full realisation of his divinity and see how he has been ensnared by matter. Although he has duties on this earth he must look way beyond it for fulfilment.

The Secret Doctrine

The occult knowledge of the esoteric schools has come up through history as the Secret Doctrine or the Ancient Wisdom or other names. This is the underlying theme, which passes on apparent inner knowledge of life. Those who belong to this tradition are called the School Men.

In Europe the tradition of the School Men began with the breakdown of the Hellenic culture, the culture of ancient Greece. The early Eleusian or even the early Christian mysteries were essentially pre-Christian in origin. They have always admitted magic, mysticism and ideas that run contrary to reason and logic. They carry the idea that there is no ultimate reality and no abiding beauty save in God and the way towards God is via the disciplines and in particular via art.

This idea got a strange impulse from the East during the Renaissance, when many scholars and artists and literary figures became initiates of the Schools, especially in Florence at the time of Marcilio Ficcino. From that school and possibly from far back beyond it come these words:

> *Artist you are a priest,*
> *Art is the great mystery;*
> *Artist you are a king,*
> *Art is the great empire.*
> *Artist you are a magus'*
> *Art is the great miracle.*

Among the many esoteric sects, which embodied schools of an esoteric kind was the so-called Prieuré de Sion. This was said to have ancient knowledge based on Jewish Gnosticism. It sprang from the Hebrew tradition. They, like many of the ancient schools in Europe, concerned themselves with the measurement of the great temple and with other measurements going right back to Pythagoras. They also had links with the Knights Templars and the Rosicrucians -- the symbol of the rose and the cross -- with their rituals and invocations. They all came in the same line. There are very many well known grand masters of the Prieuré de Sion, founded in 1090. They include Leonardo da Vinci (1452), Michelangelo, Botticelli (1444), Robert Fludd (1574), Isaac Newton, Charles Radcliffe, Chateaubriand, Victor Hugo, Claude Debussy, Jean Cocteau as late as 1889. This line has gone on as a secret underlying school, although much weakened now. And there are other similar traditions underlying society even today.

There were strong links between the Prieure de Sion and the Cathars. These early Christians were persecuted and destroyed as heretics in the thirteenth century. From this we get the word catharsis meaning 'a cleansing'. They believed in reincarnation and recognised the feminine principles. They denied the validity of the established church and of all clerical hierarchies. They disliked priests intervening between man and God. They rejected faith and insisted on personal knowledge through mystical experience. They saw a continuing war between good and evil, light and dark, spirit and matter. They saw man struggling upwards from the dark towards light and having to get control of the things of the dark. They were said to be keepers of the Holy Grail, which figures so largely in the legends of King Arthur.

Recent research in a book called 'Holy Blood and the Holy Grail' by Michael Baigent, Richard Leigh and Henry Lincoln has brought to the surface a curious offshoot of the Prieuré de Sion. The authors found some people who were said to be in a line of inheritance from Jesus and Mary Magdalen who were supposed to have had a child. There is still a family surviving in Rennes le Chateau in France, who claim to be direct descendants of this line. This is an offshoot of the true school teaching but a rather interesting and curious one.

The real school teachings were much more concerned with mathematics and with number as basic to life, with the theories of Pythagoras and the idea of growth through many lives leading to transformation of the soul. Artists of the medieval schools adopted the snail and the butterfly as symbols of the transformation of the soul and the wholeness of the individual --the snail who carries his own shell, and the butterfly born from the caterpillar. They painted them into the corners of their pictures. Many of the Old Masters have a discreet little snail or a small butterfly put in discreetly, for fellow initiates to recognise. They were saying by this means 'I know the truth, I am part of this school, I am part of the esoteric tradition.' These can be seen today if you look at old paintings or manuscripts. Sometimes you will see a small snail or butterfly even entangled in the illuminated lettering of old manuscripts. You might not see it unless you were looking for it but this was the sign of the School Man.

A great deal of school teaching in Christian times stems from Origen in Alexandria at the end of the first century. He was the son of a Greek scholar in Egypt. His father taught him Greek philosophy and then he became a Christian, which produced great tension between father and son. He was very scholarly. The Doctrine of Origen combined both Greek and Christian philosophy, including reincarnation which was declared 'anathema' in the third century, but which continued to be taught in the esoteric schools, although not outwardly in the church at all. Origen taught a great many ideas stemming from Greece: for instance that there are many gods, spirits and discarnate beings, not just a single line from Christ as the main source of attention. And the whole of the tradition of magic was recognised.

The church denounced Origen as a heretic. Among other condemned heretics was Pelagius, (380 to 420 AD), who lived in Britain. He denied 'original sin' and said that man was not born in sin or in need of redemption. He suggested we have free will and can communicate with God without benefit of priests. The whole of the Doctrine of Pelagius was declared a heresy in the late fifth century. It was, of course, 'school knowledge' and ran contrary to the authoritarianism of the established church.

The Rejected Knowledge

Heresies included all traditions which stem from Hermes Trismegistus or from Zoroaster or from Orpheus, Pythagoras or whoever, which 'ought to be rejected by society.' That is, all pseudo sciences, or inexact or incomplete sciences of occult tradition. The attraction of these teachings is discussed at length by James Webb in his book *'Flight from Reason'*. He states that 'the so-called heresies reject the bleak findings of the scientific or authoritative teaching and methods, which so often make the individual man feel so insignificant. They always hold that man is divine or capable of divinity and they assert his cosmic relevance as a power. They see power flowing through the individual.'

Madame Blavatsky, founder of the Theosophical Society, wrote an imaginary history of 12,000 years of existence in her book 'Isis Unveiled'. Her main work, 'The Secret Doctrine', published in six volumes, carries the idea of messages from ancient sources being conveyed on today by the Mahatmas in India. She believed there were ancient teachers living in the Himalayas. Some of them were actually alive in a physical form; others were discarnate beings whose ancient wisdom could be 'channelled' by a living master.

The Hermetic Order of the Golden Dawn in the late nineteenth century and Rudolf Steiner's work, and much of Gurdjieff's teaching carried knowledge from other esoteric sources. For instance, Gurdjieff brought in a great deal of material from Sufi -- that is ancient esoteric Arabian sources -- and the teachings of my brother in law Rodney Collin in his Theory of Celestial Influence carry on these ideas and bring in new scientific ideas that run alongside them.

The most interesting and well documented esoteric school was in Europe. It was that of the Neo-Platonic Academy in fifteenth century Florence. This was a period when there was a great awakening of interest in the old Greek and Roman traditions. A rich family of bankers, the Medici, collected many ancient manuscripts and even wanted to make them available to people at large. Cosimo de Medici opened the first public library in Europe, in Florence. He wanted to make knowledge available to the people, whereas the churches always wanted to keep knowledge private, and for the few who were deemed worthy of it.

In 1438 Cosimo de Medici received the Emperor of Constantinople, who was asking for financial help against Turkish invaders. He brought with him a great entourage of people. His search for practical help was in vain, for there was little forthcoming. The kingdom of Constantinople was shortly afterwards overrun. But within the court that came down from Constantinople to Florence there were School Men from the Orient. Thus knowledge of the ancient secret tradition was passed on to Cosimo di Medici and then to his grandson Lorenzo. They founded the Neo-Platonic Florentine Academy under the auspices of Marcilio Ficcino. Ficcino was given a copy of the Hermetica, which was brought by a monk from Constantinople, and he translated it into the common tongue. He believed it to be a 'great aid to religion for those who want to enquire further into the scriptures.'

Rodney Collin, when speaking of the Florentine Academy, wrote 'We can't know what took place in it but we read of gatherings at the Villa Careggi at Fiesole near Florence. And we look at paintings by Botticelli or Dosso Dossi in which the models seem to be so alert and alive that they look as though they are in a state of self-remembering. From this group, and the knowledge accumulated there, went out Politian and Mirandola to launch a literary renaissance; Botticelli and Verrocchio to create an artistic one; Reuchlin to sow the seeds of reformation in Germany; Linacre to found the Royal College of Physicians in London; Leon Battista Alberti, the grandfather of renaissance architecture, whose inspiration was the divine proportion and the Pythagoras system of numbers.

Lorenzo, (the nominal head of the Academy, after his father Cosimo died) discovered and brought up Michelangelo, and selected young Leonardo da Vinci to work in Milan.

Upon the art, technique, literature, ideals and freedom that it engendered, Western culture developed and grew and existed into living memory.

'So culture is born from culture, each fathered by some seed, some alien but esoteric source. The medieval by new knowledge from the Arab world: the renaissance by those driven west by the fall of the Byzantine; the new civilisation of our own day perhaps by the release of ancient wisdom from India and Tibet. For those concerned with the birth of a new civilisation must over and over again admit that everything in history must be reconstructed, everything made over and over again from the beginning in a new form suitable for a new age.

'Looking back from our standpoint over the descent of history, we can see that each new reality was a tremendous effort to continue. There was no beginning but only a continuation of the life of humanity. For those who had to begin to engender a new phase of human development, this beginning was a life or death matter. But from the point of view of the stars nothing was altered because humanity and all its potentials remained the same.' (*The Theory of Celestial Influence*. Rodney Collin. Arkana 1993).

The Sheep and the Goats

So those of us who are living now, at the beginning of the twenty first century, may well be conscious of the breaking down, once again, of old cultures and traditions. The social picture changes, customs alter, laws are repealed and many new ones introduced. Within living memory, society has experienced many upheavals and reversals of attitude. And yet the eternal knowledge which seems to have run through mankind's tenancy of this earth, lives still beneath the surface, cherished as an esoteric core to our understanding. Perhaps we need to try at this time, to 'make all things new' once again; and instead of preaching gloom and doom and that

Armageddon is nigh, think what we can bring back from the old traditions and use them in a practical way today.

It's worth considering that when the ancient traditions of esoteric and occult school come to the surface, as they have in this day and age, the responsibility of the individual is very markedly to the fore at the same time. The established church, or the established state, always has a certain vested interest in playing down the individual's responsibilities. The church wants all its followers to be the good sheep following the good shepherd; the church doesn't like the goats who go their own way! Out in the desert where sheep and goats run together, custom has it that there must always be one good leading goat because it is the goat who will know where it is possible to find good pasture, where there is water. The silly sheep simply trot along behind It is the goat who knows. But of course the church doesn't like the goats! They're much too difficult, and have a will of their own. The established state, likewise, quite clearly has a strong interest in making us all obey the laws and regulations that make life easier for those who put themselves in authority.

We are living now in a time of many laws and regulations, so that even the teaching in State schools has to be identical in each school, and there is to be no deviation from what is taught as 'politically correct.' When this happens, there is ultimately a rigidity and a stultification of enterprise, imagination and vision. We live in one of these periods. But in these periods too some of the old ideas of the responsibility of the individual, and indeed of God within the individual, come to the surface. We can, if we so wish, without in any way running contrary to good and decent principles, make ourselves responsible for what we believe, and for how inwardly, in privacy, we conduct our lives.

One of the things that comes to the surface each time the esoteric school ideas become available again -- and of course in many periods of time they go underground and are apparently lost, but they always resurface again sooner or later -- is the idea of the Chakras. These are concerned with what is known traditionally as the occult anatomy of man as distinct from the physical anatomy. The Chakras are vortices of energy -- the vital force system flowing through man. By tradition there is always a two-way energy flow from the crown or the Spirit to the root or the earth. The Cabalistic tree of life is much the same, as indeed is the horoscope chart in astrology which shows the energy flowing from the sun, via the moon to the earth with sevenfold influences.

So although much of the secret knowledge is lost or hard to come by, there remains available to us a number of diagrams, purporting to show the nature of life, the human body from an occult point of view, and ideas of God and of the Universe. Patterns and diagrams may be used to clarify that which is beyond words or logical explanations. The Horoscope chart, the Tree of Life of the Cabala, and the Chakras all embody remnants of school ideas, and all are used enthusiastically today by students of the occult. We may find them very helpful indeed in answering our basic questions and working towards self knowledge.

The Chakras

The Chakras suggest that all life is energy, with different rates of energy moving throughout the body from a very high and rapid vibration to a very slow and low one. It is rapid at the crown chakra of the body and slow and heavy at the root or base chakra. The idea of the descent of Spirit into matter, is understood by this. It shows a first cause casting itself out into vast energy fields. The chakras are illustrated as a simple design of a man sitting in a meditation or lotus posture, with great whirling wheels of energy above the head at the crown, at the brow, at the throat, at the heart, at the solar plexus, at the sacral area and at the base or genital area of the body.

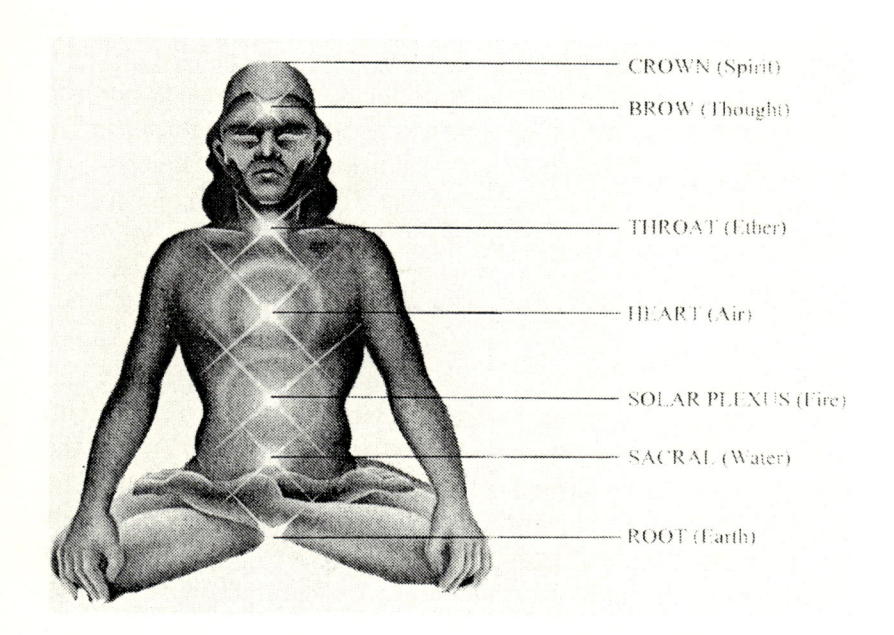

CROWN (Spirit)
BROW (Thought)
THROAT (Ether)
HEART (Air)
SOLAR PLEXUS (Fire)
SACRAL (Water)
ROOT (Earth)

The Chakras
The traditional psychic centres of the body

At the crown is said to be the Spirit above or touching the top of the head. The halo of saints or the tonsure of monks represents this chakra. At the brow is thought, or the soul. At the throat is the level of ether. All the lower elements can manifest from this level. But below this level are the four elements we know. Heart is the element of air. The solar plexus the element of fire. The sacral area is water and the root or base is the earth.

There is an energy field experienced around all living bodies. The occult anatomy theory speaks of two currents, positive and negative, always crossing at the nodal points between each of the Chakras. The positive is called the Pingala and the negative is the Ida. Between the two, running up and down, is the Sushumna. The Tree of Life equivalent is the two columns of force and form and we will deal with that later in this book.

The root or base Chakra (Earth) is sometimes shown at the level of the feet but more often it indicates the genital area; this is energy at its 'grossest' but often strongest level -- sex energy from which all finer and more refined forms of energy spring. The sacral area (Water), all the waters of the body, the kidneys, the liver, the digestive system are all seen at this point. The Solar Plexus (Fire) is the next area. Of course solar means the Sun: warmth, joviality, expansion and enjoyment. At the heart area (Air) is said to be sympathy lightness and joy. Here are the four elements, which we have and with which we must live because our whole bodies depend on the interplay of those elements within the physical body.

Above this we are dealing with rather shaky ideas of ether or space, thought and Spirit. Cheirology, which we mentioned in the previous chapter, lumps all three of the higher energies together in the head area, only acknowledging the four base elements as far as the throat. But the tradition of the Chakras defines the higher elements much more clearly and suggests that our object should be to open the Chakras in such a way as to ensure that the higher elements have full play.

If we are feeling insecure, up in the top Chakras, we need to be earthed. Officialdom tends however to be stuck at the lower level, not wanting to budge, crystallised down there in a very slow level of movement and being! Which is why one has the bureaucrat saying 'I don't make the laws, I only carry them out. It's more than my job's worth to break the rules'. There is no thought here, but only a mechanical churning out and repeating the obvious. We need to be conscious at all levels. From the 'gross' to the 'subtle': that is the very fine, light, rapid energy at the highest level . We may be able to work via the Chakras, as we look towards understanding of ourselves, body, mind and Spirit.

The opening and closing of the Chakras is an occult practice. Normally we go through life with them closed. In special situations such as healing or counselling, they may open naturally and many therapists deliberately attempt this. But it can make people very vulnerable if their Chakras are all open. Normally they will probably open and close automatically. For instance, the lower Chakras will probably open automatically in times of anger, desperation. Or during sexual arousal. The higher Chakras tend only to be opened by will and attention.

Attempting to open and close the Chakras is an act of the mind: it has just about as much, or possibly as little, 'reality' as the programming of a crystal to make it serve our purpose. As we are dealing with occult anatomy rather than physical anatomy we can't be sure what, if anything, is actually happening if we try to open or close the Chakras. It's part of occult tradition that something can happen. If we pay attention to the different parts of the body, with these whirling vortices of energy with the Pingala running on the right and the Ida on the left (but crossing over in between each Chakra), we can awaken in our imagination the idea of a continual state of movement, development and flow. This can be done as an action of meditation. We can become conscious of it.

The Rainbow Spectrum

The Chakras are associated also with colour: the colours of the spectrum, in exactly the same order as the colours of the rainbow. At the base the Chakra is red; at the sacral area it is orange; at the solar plexus is the gold colour of the sun -- the solar plexus related to the sun; at the heart level green; at the level of the throat blue or purple as related to the spectrum; indigo at the brow; violet at the crown.

The colours of the spectrum are, of course, red, orange, yellow, green, blue, indigo and violet. The primary colours red, yellow and blue, are interspersed by the secondary colours or the mixture of the one above and one below. Red + yellow = orange. Yellow + blue = green. Blue + red = indigo or violet. So if you are visualising the Chakras, it is a good idea to visualise them as being bathed in colour. The colours of the spectrum are very important and are bound to come in many other places in our study of esoteric matters.

In attempting to open the Chakras, we can open from the crown downwards and then close by starting from the base Chakra and moving up. This is to bring the power of the crown -- that area of rapid vibration -- down through all the other Chakras, and closing it again. Or you may prefer to start with the base Chakra, move up to the crown and then down to the base again. The object of using the Chakras and meditating upon them is to become conscious of the balance within one's own body.

If you know yourself well already then you will already know whether you tend to be a predominantly earthy person, watery, fiery or airy. And you may realise that there tends to be more strength in that part of the body which is relevant for your particular element. But of course we don't need only the passion of the root, or the fine vibrations of the crown, to be fully balanced people. We need to be conscious of all the Chakras and aware that they ought to work together in harmony, opening and closing according to our own will and attention.

Kundalini Energy

By tradition the opening of the Chakras can also result in the raising of the Kundalini, which is the enormously strong life force rising via the spinal column. It is sometimes called the serpent energy. The raising of the Kundalini is essentially a 'school' practice and it is not advisable as a rule for the individual student to attempt to do this. It can result in a very extreme state of sexual arousal, as tremendous energy seems to flow from the genital area up throughout the body towards the crown of the head.

In this book, although I mention occult practices, I also

mention a slight warning not to go too far. It's a good idea to be conscious of the Chakras but not a very good idea to go into strongly-motivated or strong-willed attempts to open the Chakras in such a way that the Kundalini power may be raised. It is not necessary for us. Working with the Chakras, like working with the Cabala or the Horoscope or the Tarot cards, or any of the other occult sciences that we mention in this book, are all part of the very useful wealth of scholarly knowledge belonging to the school of rejected ideas. If we come across these ideas and wish to use them, we are at liberty to do so. But as each of us travels alone, a little caution is needed. Alertness and attention to what we are doing should never be forgotten. If we are rightly motivated we will grow in stature and understanding with the years.

Suggested Exercises

1) Meditate on the Chakras. Sit quietly and attentively, with your eyes closed. Transfer you attention from outer things to your own body. Begin with the base Chakra. Put your mind on the enormous energy, which lies at the base of the spine and the genital area. Visualise a clear red light. Move up in your attention to the sacral area. See the light change to orange and consider the digestive system of your body. Move up from there to the solar plexus. See the golden yellow of the sun and be conscious of warmth. Move up from there to the heart. See the light change to green. Feel your heartbeat. Visualize the great heartbeat of life. Move up to the throat. See the green light change to blue/purple of the etheric level. Move on to the brow level, seeing the light turn into indigo at the level of thought, and let this be the higher thought of this high vibrating level where there is no violence or passion but almost silence. And finally to the crown level touching or above the head and be conscious here of beautiful violet light at that highest level. After a pause, bring yourself down again through the rainbow spectrum, and open your

eyes when you are ready.

This is a safe and pleasant contemplation of the Chakras that can make you aware of how your body functions and where your consciousness tends to be seated within your occult anatomy. It is generally sufficient to practice in this way.

2) In a state of meditation, ponder on the word discipline. What does it mean to you?

5

Angels and Archangels

Most cultures have some sort of belief in discarnate intelligences, heavenly beings or an angelic kingdom. The Hebrew tradition defines the angelic kingdom very clearly. The angels and archangels whose names we tend to know, like Michael, Gabriel and Raphael, all stem from the ancient Biblical tradition. Their attributes and functions are discussed in the Old Testament. But in other periods of time and different civilisations there's been the belief that discarnate presences of some kind may be encountered as guides or as messengers, who convey important knowledge, or bring communications from people we may have loved in this life and who may have died before us.

It seems a good idea to look at the whole question of carnate or discarnate lives and what we mean by this. Carnate means of course in fleshly form: *carne* the flesh as distinct from the Spirit.

The whole subject of angels, archangels and the elemental kingdom is so enormous that we need to look at it and consider very deeply what we personally may think and believe on these subjects. So much of our understanding and personal growth may depend on how much contemplation and meditation we put into this matter: whether we really believe in intelligences or 'presence's' which are discarnate--that is, not in a physical form. You may feel very aware of such presences. I am myself. Even in childhood I would feel perhaps somebody is in the room, or with me. Angels or fairies, or even people who had died, seemed sometimes to just 'be around'. Occasionally I would think they had something to tell me. But usually I couldn't really hear anything. As I grew older I wondered about trying to invoke them.

There are very few clear cut definitions which explain the subject of invoking and evoking a 'presence' of some kind. There can be the impression that there's not much difference between the sort of guardian angel-cum-fairy godmother who may be spoken to and can perhaps help us, or a voice coming through a medium who says: 'I have your mother here and she would like to speak to you'; or even the great archangels we were taught about as children. They may sometimes be lumped together in people's consciousness with all the other discarnate voices and intelligences, as though they all live at the other side of a curtain or veil while we live on this side on earth. I want to put before you the ancient idea that men and women may be very few and that the discarnate realms are enormous.

The elemental kingdoms are tied to this planet and are below the real level and potential of mankind. They might be evoked by chance if we are not careful; but as I have mentioned before, it is important not to be at their mercy. We should not be commanded by them. The angels and archangels, however, may be invited or invoked, which is quite a different matter. The life principles personified by the angels are very much tied up with the ancient traditions of occult knowledge, such as the Major Arcana of the Tarot cards or the planetary principles in Astrology.

The old Hebrew structure, which can be found in the Old Testament and in many other ancient documents of holy writ, says there are a number of angels and archangels which are all attendant on the Lord God. Around such archangels there are enormous 'hosts' of angels, which carry out the bidding of the great archangels.

According to Hebrew traditions the separate intelligences that were created during the six days that brought the cosmos into being, are divided between those that dwell in the celestial region and those that dwell in the terrestrial region: the elementals. The will of God operates throughout but mankind alone has the right to go up or down. It is as if the Universe itself requires a species that can move and grow, a species of being having free will. The angels hold their same positions for ever, and can't evolve, for they have their duty to do, and no freewill, just as the elementals have no free will.

Angelic Grace

According to this tradition, sometimes the angels may help us, by grace. By grace they may heal our wounds. But no matter how much we may try to evoke or pray to them we are not likely to attract the attention of the highest, the archangels. But we may attract the attention of one of the minions or hosts of the archangels. That is, the attendant angels who conform to the particular archetypal principles that we are asking for: i.e. for knowledge, for healing or for help in one way or another.

It's useful to consider which group we ourselves are attracted to. The hosts of the angels have some of the characteristics of the archangels to whom they belong. We seem to be evolving They seem to 'keep their ancient places'. They appear to be there, according to this idea, to praise the Lord, to say something like 'all is love'; 'all can be healed'; 'cherish the earth'; 'by grace you may ascend'; 'here is knowledge'; 'repent of your sins'. Each Archangel stands for an enormous principle, and all his/its minions stand for the same principle that he/it stands for. Angels appear to be androgynous: i.e. neither male nor female.

Although there are a great number of angels and archangels mentioned in the Bible and other ancient texts, broadly speaking the ones we recognise are these:

                    Metatron

    Zaphkiel   Raziel

    Samael   Zadkiel

                    Michael

    Raphael   Haniel

                    Gabriel

                   Sandolphon

Central is Michael, host of the chief archangels, and said to be 'like unto God'. He can communicate with those above and with those below. Churches are often dedicated to St Michael and All Angels, thus indicating this high status.

Then looking down to the bottom of the diagram I have given you we see Sandolphon, the guardian spirit of all beings. Above him Gabriel, the enormous archangel who stands for spiritual knowledge and who can assist us with all knowledge and understanding. He and his hosts are always crying 'here is knowledge' He can be the messenger who can bring us the help we need. If you get hooked on the idea of getting more knowledge you are plugged into the Gabriel line!

Above him appear a pair of angels who seem to be balancing each ,other. Raphael on the left, who stands for healing. He is said to be the divine physician. He heals mankind, the universe and anything or anyone who is in distress. On the other side, balancing him, Haniel who stands for the grace of God. He may occasionally be received 'by grace', but not by right. These two appear to balance each other so that we may indeed be healed by grace.

Michael, Lord of Hosts, is above: and then another pair Samael and Zadkiel. Samael on the left stands for the severity of God, the guardian of evil; here is the principle of the ferocious God of the Old Testament of whom the Jews lived in such fear and were always trying to placate him. Zadkiel, balancing him, stands for the benevolence of God, the guardian of good.

Above is another pair: Zaphkiel the contemplation of God, and balancing him Raziel the revelation of God. These are the heralds of the deity, the guardians of the secrets of God. As you see, there is a growth in subtlety and refinement of thought as one approaches the godhead itself.

Above these, very high indeed, comes Metatron, the great Archangel of the Presence of the Lord. Known as the Archangel of the Presence, he is the guardian of the doorway.

Guardian of the Doorway

You see how these are showing a developing system rising from what we can easily understand as our own need for help, healing, knowledge and so on to a level where anyone quietly and deeply contemplating, should begin to experience awe, hesitation, reverence perhaps. What is beyond the doorway? Have I any right to enter? Can I even enter or is it beyond comprehension to us?

When I ask you to work on yourselves, to contemplate these things, you will realise that nothing I can say or write can give you an experience of any of this enormous developing scale. To become a man/woman of knowledge, we have to look into it for ourselves.

Around each archangel there is an enormous host of angels carrying out the bidding of the archangel. As you pray or ponder, you may well attract the attention of some Being up there. But none of the angels and archangels are complete in themselves. They are part of an enormous whole. Those who get hooked on 'all is love' and want to heal everyone may well be hooked into the Raphael host for instance, while as I have already mentioned, those who thirst for knowledge may attract the attention of the hosts of Gabriel. These are all part of the great, ancient pattern of the angelic kingdoms, which exist above the earthly level, in discarnate state.

Man has the function, the possibility, to go back to the Lord of All. In the opening book of the Bible, Genesis, it says that Man is made in God's own image and therefore has free will. He is left to roam freely. There is only one law and that is not to eat of the tree of the knowledge of good and evil. In the legend of the fall from grace and the expulsion from the Garden of Eden we see how Adam and Eve use their free will, not just to bask in the glory, but to find out what it is all about. They become aware of what they are and so are cast out of the Garden of Eden. So the role of man is much more difficult than that of the angels, or of the elemental kingdom of the plants and flowers and trees in the Garden.

The angels and archangels by tradition, know something of the future. We may invoke them, for they have an enabling function to see that the pattern is fulfilled, that the universe is in balance. Warren Kenton, the Cabalist, who writes as Z'ev ben Shimon Halevi says 'As the great ray of creation descends, life gets more and more involved.' Lower down the scale, he suggests, the hosts control and tend to manipulate events, but they have no intimate knowledge of the Lord themselves. They are too far away. They are incomplete beings and may even have conflicting interests, limited by their own role. Balance is maintained by the hosts of Michael, who predominates in the long run in all conflicts from below. There are lots of minor angels with smaller and smaller functions.

Whole armies of angels are required at the lower levels, to develop the process of evolution. To evolve further we ourselves must understand the whole enormous pattern and not get hooked on one only of the archangels because we may then go on repeating and repeating one particular role through many lives. This would cut out many of our inherent possibilities.

A Different Approach

Apart from the quite well known table of Archangels above, there are other, equally ancient diagrams, such as this:

North
Uriel
Earth
(Oldest)

West	East
Gabriel	Raphael
Water	Air
(Older)	(Young, Fair)

South
Michael
Fire
(Mature)

Here we are offered only four Archangels, and they are set out in a different order. They read round the points of the compass from East, to South, then West and lastly North. Raphael, the first is shown as young and very fair, and associated with the element Air. Michael is a little older, a little less fair, and is associated with Fire. Gabriel is shown as more mature, darker, associated with Water. And finally at the North comes Uriel, the oldest and darkest of them all, and associated with Earth. Uriel is not mentioned at all in the other table.

From this apparent contradiction, you may perhaps surmise that it is not so much the positioning or particular attributes of individual angels which we need to consider. It is the whole question of what the angelic kingdom may be, what we understand by it. If we think in terms of deep and fundamental archetypal forces, we may see how they appear to manifest themselves in such a way that some understanding of their nature may be 'picked up' by mankind -- but perhaps understood slightly differently in different ages and cultures. In Western culture they may appear as an Archangel, the Madonna or the Christ. In other cultures perhaps as many, many gods, spirits or daemons.

Visions and Apparitions

Manifestations of this kind are found for instance at Fatima or Medjugorje. It is interesting to pay attention to these visions and apparitions at such well known shrines, some of which have appeared in our own time. Thousands flock to a hillside where a beautiful lady has been seen usually believed to be an angel or the Madonna, usually by children in the first instance. The 'lady' gives messages usually that mankind must repent in order to be saved. It is important to pay attention to this sort of thing because it has some kind of reality.

I think myself that these manifestations may come from Uriel because Uriel appears as a dark angel whose main function is to do with guilt, penance, repentance, shame, grief, and very often an indication of dire things to come. So the manifestation of the Madonna, presenting itself first as loving and gentle, always has this sting in the tail. Medjugorje is particularly interesting in that she not only has appeared for some years, but during the Bosnian fighting, many people flocked to this area, which is in the seat of the war zone in the Balkans, always to hear the voice telling them how wicked man is and how we must all turn back to God or suffer the consequences. It is also interesting that Medjugorje was never bombed or fought over. Many people felt the area was in some way 'protected.' There was certainly power there.

It seems probable that while the angels and archangels repeat and repeat a particular theme, a particular mantra as it were, mankind has the possibility to be conscious of and to invoke all the principles and possibly alter the pattern of events in his own life to some extent.

In the book 'The only Planet of Choice' edited by Palden Jenkins, from channelled messages through an American medium Phyllis Schlemmer, there is a suggestion that man by his own will can choose to go back to the source instead of repeating on and on and remaining in one place like the angels.

Angels have a very important function, Jenkins suggests, but they are not enough in themselves. What is important is understanding which involves being aware of the whole picture. Real individual growth involves this understanding or at least the beginnings of it and this is where our own possibilities come in.

Many people in this day and age believe they have experienced the presence of angels or have received messages from them. Of course here we are in the same realm of individual belief and experience as we are when we think of fairies in the woods, nature spirits or a diva that may control a garden or a hillside. Namely we are in realms that we may loosely call imagination. In other words it is not by the intellect but by the senses that we have these experiences.

It is important to think where we stand relative to the vast range of intelligence's that we are talking about. We may by chance or luck, or as a result of some action of our own evoke or encounter something that may be associated solely with this Earth. If we are looking for an aid to understanding or help of a higher nature we are looking above our own level. We need to approach not only with caution, but with such respect or reverence as we may find to be appropriate when we are looking toward the godhead. It seems fitting to ask for help rather than to demand it and to know that if it comes it comes by grace from a higher level than our own. So therefore acknowledgement and thanks appears to be appropriate.

If we yearn deeply for higher knowledge we may well be looking to the hosts of Gabriel to bring us within reach of the right books, the right instructors, the best teacher to help us at this time. For Gabriel is the great communicator, the bearer of knowledge.

If on the other hand we are more concerned with healing the world and the people in it we may be much more drawn to the hosts of Raphael who deals with all matters of distress. All sincere healers are surely aided by the hosts of Raphael. So those who think in terms of 'love and peace' 'all is love' and who long to help are deeply drawn to this archetype or angelic being.

We look very high indeed if we look for St. Michael and All Angels for although well known and recognised by mankind, St. Michael is very far above us. He/It is an enormous power that we might invoke at our peril unless we are of great integrity and honesty of intent.

All the things that we may do in dealing with 'presences' that we evoke by chance or which we are trying to look at consciously or those higher presence's which we can attempt to invoke asking for their assistance, are always in the realm of experiences private to us individually. We ourselves need to decide whether we should encourage or turn away from what has appeared in our minds. No-one can make a categorical statement that we can make such higher contacts, or that they have reality; but if we think that they may have, and we look consciously and with honesty towards them we may well be surprised at the experiences that we get!

The doorway into realms of higher knowledge does occasionally open to the earnest seeker. He/she must then work on the knowledge received and make it his/her own in some way.

Guides and Helpers

Many people are so fascinated by the idea of discarnate beings that they court the idea of a guide or helper personal to themselves. There are many mediums and clairvoyants who will be delighted to encourage anyone who feels this need.

The natural or spontaneous experience, or feeling of a benevolent or loving presence, especially in times of distress or dismay, is fairly common place. And there are an enormous number of authenticated cases of those who feel that they have seen or heard a guiding presence or guardian angel bringing words of reassurance.

But it does seem important, in my opinion, not to accept a guide without question. Don't just take the word of someone who says you have a guide giving you specific messages. They may say he is Chinese and called Chan or an American Indian called Red eagle or White Feather or whatever. This can be very exciting but it often leads later on to an enormous number of doubts or confusion and sometimes even to fear. If you feel that you do need a guide then set about finding one for yourself. I'll give you some hints as to what you might do about this. Remember that the medium who gives you a guide has somehow picked up something connected with you in some way, but this may not lead you where you want to go. It may side-track you or even lead you backwards into ideas that you have outgrown. So beware too great credulity where other people's advice is concerned. Find out for yourself if possible.

Some people don't have any sense of needing a guide at all. You may wish to go straight ahead according to your own intelligence and own will, increasing your own knowledge and understanding as you travel, and being conscious of any pitfalls on the long path. But if you need help and feel you can ask for it within the realm of discarnate beings, I believe it's quite legitimate to explore in this direction.

You might find yourself drawn to any of the well known lines of those who 'channel' messages from other levels or worlds. There are many reputable channellers such as Ruth White who channels a being she knows as Gildas who gives messages of general benefit. Madame Blavatsky channelled messages attributed to Koot Hoomi or Kut Humi, and the Mahatmas in the Himalayas, who were said to provide messages about ancient civilisations as well as possibilities about the future. The White Eagle Lodge had a channelled source and a sincere church with a large following. Phyllis Schlemmer channels a group known as the Council of Nine, nine beings who claim to have lived on earth and who produce useful scientific data for the future. The Society for the Study of Spiritual Science at Diss in Norfolk, are producing channelled sources dedicated to discovering more clearly what channelling is. They certainly get some interesting physical phenomena such as swinging lamps and moving objects during their sessions!

There may be a possibility of making contact with discarnate beings and intelligences of people who have been on this earth. But I think we must be wary of trying to invoke guides or masters, just for the sake of trying to get someone to come along and give a hand. There are obvious dangers of getting into realms of fantasy when we do this, or of getting hooked on the idea of it. However a little assistance, one way or another, might be useful at this stage especially if you have been along to a Spiritualist church and heard a medium channelling someone's relative who has 'passed over' for instance and have been intrigued but not all together convinced. The messages heard by this means, often do seem to be rather trite.

If you want to try channelling for yourself, do it cautiously. Nobody has to do this of course.

A System of Channelling

A good and useful modern authority is Catherine Rydell, an American psychologist who seems very reasonably sound. She suggests that it seems more possible now than in previous times for people to contact intelligences other than ourselves. Provided one is fairly sure what one is doing and where one is going these can be of enormous help, not only for us as individuals but also for planet earth itself, Catherine Rydell says. She writes: 'We may never know for sure whether channelling is the reaction of our own minds or whether it is true communication with other beings or a way of accessing non physical energy to which we attribute a personality. But if we do invent all these channels, then the human mind has a capacity to access wisdom far beyond our conscious awareness; and if we haven't made it up then the universe may be full of many other beings who want to help us. Channelling is one of the ways to reach out beyond ordinary, sensory experience.'

She has a very sensible, practical technique which seems to work and be very safe. It consists of accepting that we all want friendship, support, wisdom, learning, teaching etc. If we could make contact with a being or beings individual to ourselves who answer our own need, we might if we wish call that person a guide, a spirit guide, a teacher, a mentor or whatever we wish. But we must first of all be sure who or what we want to contact.

She suggests that we should first ponder three simple questions and write down what is wanted. Then make a simple invocation and get into a state of quiet meditative contemplation and see if what we have got clearly in our minds can actually open the door for us.

The questions she suggests are:
1. What do I individually want to know and what do I want to learn from a guide?
2. What qualities do I want in my guide?
3. What sort of relationship do I want to have with my guide?

For the first question, make a list of the most important goals in your life. You might find you want to write pages and pages whereas others may only write two or three lines. This can be a mixture of the mundane or the more spiritual. For the second question you might want your guide to be serious or intellectual or humorous or light hearted or even a bit of a joker. You might want someone quite different from yourself;

you might want somebody who will clarify things if you get a bit muddled, who will give insight into wisdom or help you to be more loving or more kind etc. For the third question, 'What sort of contact do you want with your guide?' You might want a friend, a mentor, a teacher or a genuine guide to be absolutely honest. Showing your strengths and weaknesses; to be wise and understanding on spiritual matters, to be loving etc. to be able to communicate with you verbally or to whom you can pick up in some way in your own life.

Define clearly whether you are asking for a teacher, a friend or a confidante or whether you are quite content just with a guide or helper. Then get it down to a simple invocation something like this.

'I am calling to myself a spirit friend who can help me to find my own creative direction; or who has lived on earth and knows how difficult it is to deal with children for instance; or who nurtures and supports me etc.'

Make it very clear so that you don't open yourself to any entity which might want to come in. You want to get a channel open to higher things.

You can't do all this in a hurry. You might need to work on it for several days writing and rewriting the answers to your questions until you feel it's really succinct. Rydell then suggests that you sign it and date it and say it aloud two or three times. Even say it aloud every day for several days. This is almost like a radio station sending out signals and waiting for the signal to be picked up. Sit in a state of physical, emotional and mental relaxation to do this and wait a little.

Invoking a Spirit Mentor

As a personal comment, I attempted this method several years ago and got rather interesting results myself. For Rydell's three questions I wrote:

Goals
1. I would like to know more about the nature and possibilities of Man: that is my aim;
2. I would like to be given further help to develop towards cosmic consciousness;
3. I would like to be given clear purpose and aid in attempting to help others who come to my classes or to a group in my house;
4. I would like to prepare for death as a fulfilment rather than an end.

Under *Qualities*, I wrote. To have religious and scientific knowledge above my own very limited knowledge. To want to talk to me; to be able to cause events leading onto greater fulfilment and happiness; to help to give good counsel and honest guidance to those who come to me for Tarot readings, Astrology and so on; and to be clearly of honest and honourable intent.

Then under the relationship that I wanted with my guide I wrote. To give me a strong sense of purpose and a feeling that help is always available; to impinge on my consciousness at times of stress or distress and calm and encourage me; to be a wise counsellor and friend but not to have ultimate control over me.

Then I worded the invocation as this: 'I am calling to myself a spirit mentor, who has greater knowledge of the nature and possibilities of man, who wants to talk to me and will be a supporter and a counsellor' and I signed and dated it.

When you are ready to try and begin to invoke and get a response, choose a time when you know you will be alone and undisturbed; sit upright with your feet on the floor and your back straight and your hands relaxed, your whole body relaxed. Feel the earth beneath your feet, feel your body, your face, your neck, your shoulders, your hands. Relaxed, upright and comfortable, breathe deeply. Quiet breathing. Be aware of your breath, inhaling and exhaling from deep down in your stomach. Breathe in and imagine pulling vital white energy in which rejuvenates you and gives you a deep sense of calm. Breathe out imagining yourself relieving the stresses and tensions of the day, the negativity. Feel the weight of gravity pulling you down, connecting you to the earth and pay attention to your creative energy. At your own natural speed, as slow as is comfortable, breathe in vital energy calming and rejuvenating and breathe out the negativity.

Now when you are ready, begin to imagine two or three feet in front of you, a vessel, a bowl or a cup: a chalice or a container of some kind which is beautiful and strong. Take time to visualise it clearly; see its detail, what it is made of; its colour, inside and outside are they the same? Imagine it coming closer and closer until you yourself merge with it; you yourself are the vessel. Describe it to yourself using the first person.

You are a vessel. Experience your own boundaries or walls; experience the sides of the vessel. Feel yourself a strong container, ready to hold many things. Experience yourself as the inside, the receptive openness, waiting to be filled. Experience your own strong boundaries, your own willingness to be a receptive vessel. Use this vessel technique to create yourself as a grounded vessel to take the expanded energies of your guide or your higher self. With the rather nebulous idea you already have of what you want to experience and the memory of what you are asking for, sit merged with your vessel trying to feel an answering response. This will become more marked when you make your invocation. But on the first occasion just close or cover the vessel after you have struggled like this and have got some feeling of making the vessel and becoming the vessel. Move yourself away from it as you cover or close the vessel, so you become a separate entity again. Then on the next occasion, when you begin, go as far as making your invocation and waiting.

Now to pursue this idea you will need to give time, not only to write out your hopes and expectations and to get a short invocation that you can memorise. You also need to follow the meditation that I have just given you. People have very different reactions; some get an increased flow of energy, they may feel vibrations throughout their whole body, or just in part of their body, or a feeling of expansion from the top of the head. Or a feeling as though some of the Chakras are being activated. You could get visual images. Whatever it is that happens, it is a response to the call that you have sent out. Guides come in a great many different ways to different individuals so you might want to practice on a number of different days, waiting until you begin to feel a presence.

Unwanted Guides

If and when you feel a presence, if it is the sort of guide you have asked for try the following technique. I am quoting very much from Catherine Rydell who has so much experience of this technique which I feel to be good and sound. It's important not to accept the feeling of a guide or presence whom you don't want. You can very reasonably say inwardly 'go away, I don't want you, thank you very much for coming but go'. Now pretend that you yourself are a guide and talk as if you yourself were sitting opposite and talking to yourself. You might well say something like 'Well Joyce, I see you are finding it strange and you're not sure whether you are making it all up, or whether there's any value in this, now try to relax with it and trust me.'

This will help you to move away from your own perspective and into the perspective of the guide, even if you find yourself answering back, speaking as your guide 'Well you are a doubting Thomas! You don't really believe any of this do you? Are you really interested in getting a guide?' Then say 'Yes of course I want a guide. I am sorry if I am doubting but I think it's legitimate to be doubting.' Then as the guide 'trust a little more and wait a little more.' Then as yourself 'Well I know I'm impatient but I'm really not sure what I'm trying to do,' etc. etc. By this means, which is a simple psychological way of looking at your thoughts and ideas, moving as though into someone sitting opposite you and then back into yourself, you begin to get the feeling of how this system can work.

If you find you are losing contact and your mind is just wandering off and you think there is nobody there any more, then come back to the basic idea and find the vessel again. Make the vessel again, be the vessel again, merge with it and so deepen your meditation again. You might find you get no result or just a vague feeling when you try again, but if you persevere, you will in the end get a sense of reality behind it. Then you might reasonably have a dialogue like this 'Is there anybody there? Have you got a name? What world do you live in? How are you connected to me?' Speak the answers aloud until you feel a healthy contact. Be sure about honesty and integrity and so on.

Address your own doubts, as you will certainly feel as if you are making it all up! Experience of the inner world is very subtle and delicate, therefore persevere and you will eventually feel something new. Some things which come through will be so wise and true that you needn't really concern yourself about whether you are making it up or not. Maybe it comes from your higher self. How do you know?

Creating a Vision

Channelling is only of use if it seems to provide help for yourself. In the long run it could well provide help for the whole planet as people begin to look into this idea of contact with higher and subtler worlds. You are using your own skill and your own ability to open up to these links with inner worlds. Catherine Rydell says 'This is a time to create a vision, a dream for ourselves and for the world. This is a time of great unfolding for this planet. Old institutions, old societies, old customs are crumbling away but a new era is beginning.'

I don't for one moment want to suggest that it is essential to do an experiment like this in order to grow in wisdom, consciousness and understanding. But I think it is a very legitimate experiment that we can make following this wise guidance by an experienced psychologist. I am sure it is a perfectly safe method, if practised with moderation and if you don't get hooked on the idea of guides to the exclusion of everything else.

Remember the difference between invocation and evocation. We invoke that which is above ourselves, inviting the presence of beings above our own level. But we may find that we evoke beings which we have not invited from the elemental level or at our own level. Mankind has his own position, not right at the top of the ladder, not right at the bottom of the ladder, but not very high up either: above the elemental kingdom which is tied to this earth and below that which is of the entire solar system and the cosmos.

If we evoke, we may draw up all sorts of little beings which have something to say! We are at liberty to command or dismiss, or we may listen to them cautiously, but if in doubt say 'Goodbye, go to your own rightful place.' Evoking just happens when beings arrive uninvited. They may of course come from your own mind or from the collective unconscious. They may appear recognisably to be people who have lived on this earth or even people known to yourself who have died before you. Only you can decide whether you want to communicate with them or not.

You may conceivably fall into a light trance state if you do this and try to become the vessel, opening yourself in this way. There is absolutely no need to go into a deep trance state. You are perfectly safe when you are aware of being in a light trance and you can come out of it at will.

As a matter of personal comment, when I was experimenting in this way, I felt ultimately that I had contacted a medieval Jewish Sufi with connections with Southern France and Southern Spain. I felt that I had a very clear cut character of a highly intelligent, highly strung man who had in his own lifetime desperately wanted to talk about the things that had interested him deeply. But his colleagues and his friends were not sufficiently deeply and continually interested in him, and were inclined to be bored when he began to talk. So nervous energy was continually bubbling out of him and not finding an easy outlet.

I began eventually to visualise him as being of small stature and of having some kind of skin complaint, because he tended to scratch himself as he was talking. I could see him quite clearly. However, although I realised he had a great deal of knowledge that could be of value to me, I couldn't help him to impart it to me. It was exasperating to feel that he wanted to tell me and was aware of something linking us across time and space -- namely my desire to know and his urgent desire to tell me.

Eventually my attention was drawn to Solomon ben Gabirol (1021-1058) who was indeed a Jewish Sufi from Southern Spain and who could speak and write Arabic. He left a number of writings, complex and very profound documents, about his thoughts regarding the nature of God, about life and about Man.

When I heard Gabirol's name I felt a sense of reality as though this was indeed the man I had been talking to, although I had never heard of him before. Later on I was able to have access to modern versions of his writings which I took on board as being extremely interesting. He wrote in Arabic a document called 'The Fount of Life', which was translated into Latin a century or so after his death. His teaching was accepted by the Franciscans. He was known by the 'pen name' of Avicebron. However eventually I felt that this contact was no longer satisfactory. He was becoming increasingly more importunate, too oppressing. I then became unsure whether I was dealing with Gabirol or with somebody else, because I got the name Hugo, and then Monseigneur as though he were a Catholic priest. The two presences seemed to intermingle and I was no longer sure what I was dealing with. I felt it was possible that a Catholic priest, known by the title Monseigneur and with the first name of Hugo might have come across Gabirol's work and studied it, perhaps many years after Gabirol's death. I kept up this interesting experiment on and off for some months but finally I let it go because I felt nothing more of value could come of it.

Other people whom I have known who have practised Catherine Rydell's technique, have been comforted to feel the presence of a loved Mother or Grandfather or a known friend, or have felt something quite simple and helpful and been pleased to continue with it. If the idea appeals it's always worth having a try.

Suggested Exercises

1) If you have ever experienced a discarnate and/or possibly angelic presence, ponder it again after considering this chapter.

2) If the experiment in channelling appeals to you, practise and develop it bit by bit until you begin to get a definite result.

6

Working with the Senses

'I am a child of Earth and of the starry Heavens. But my race is of Heaven.' So, it is believed, said Pythagoras, who lived in about 500bc.

We've spent a lot of time so far discussing discarnate beings at a level below man, (the elementals) and in the Angelic Kingdom and up towards the Godhead itself. We ourselves fit in somewhere. We may perhaps think, because of our fleshly form and yet our apparent yearning for God, that we are beings of spirit in a material form.

Sometimes it may almost feel as though we are trapped in this heavy body. That the flesh, which both sustains us and enables us to live and eat and grow and to use our senses in this world, also holds us in thrall in a vale of troubles and woes and difficulties. And it would be so nice to get out of it! As Shakespeare said 'O that this too too solid flesh would melt.'

To struggle against the body, however, trying to subdue it or punish it as many religious people have done in the past, seems fairly pointless. In the same way it seems a waste to use the physical body in a promiscuous, self indulgent way which doesn't keep it healthy or strong or clean. Because our physical body is such a marvellous piece of work, we need to appreciate it and use the potential of the body. Of course the body not only sustains us, but can be of great joy to us. It is our means, our vehicle to get around in this world, so we'd better maintain it well!

To understand the body and live in it fully, and to understand the need to develop oneself via the body, seems to me to be the way to go forward. For people like us, who are mostly never going to be monks or nuns or ascetics. And who probably don't want to be 'drop outs' on the whole either, self-remembering, self-observation, and paying attention to the body seems to be very important from the point of view of growth of consciousness.

But also we need to aspire beyond the body. So we need to stretch ourselves beyond the ordinary experiences which come via the senses.

Everything we experience of this world we do via the five senses: sight, hearing, taste, touch and smell. They are our media. But they may also be guardians, which prevent us from being overwhelmed in some way and almost descending into madness by too many impressions. The quotation at the beginning of this book explains this in that way: '.........perhaps our frames could hardly bear much of it' if we really experienced the world fully. '........If we had a keen vision and feeling of all ordinary human life, it would be like hearing the grass grow and the squirrel's heartbeat, and we should die of that roar which lies on the other side of silence.' This is of course from George Elliott's 'Middlemarch'.

Until we start really observing, we're hardly aware either how limited is our usual perception, or how much there is beyond the ordinary senses. We seem to need our very limited senses as a kind of barrier. Schizophrenia is said to be the result of uncontrollable perception, too much can be seen and experienced. As you know, some schizophreniacs are very talented and can paint beautifully, can write strange poetry, are skilled musicians and have extraordinary insight. But uncontrollable perception apparently makes one mad. So, if we're going to develop our senses beyond the very narrow range that we are used to, we need to go cautiously! But with conscious attention we can go safely into the unknown worlds. Instead of dying of 'the roar' or turning away in fear from the unknown, thinking it is all too much, we may begin to detect within the apparent chaos a sweet, harmonious music. Perhaps the music of the spheres.

The Five Basics

First of all, consider the five ordinary senses.

Sight. If our sight is normal, we can perceive things providing they are within a certain size range or within a certain distance. If something is too big we can't see what it is. It's almost like touching the side of an elephant and being aware of grey rough skin -- not realising because it is so big that it is actually an elephant with a tail at one end and a trunk at the other. We simply can't observe what is too big. And if a thing is too small we may not be able to see what it is or even to see it at all. We need a microscope to observe tiny particles.

An easy way to grasp this is to consider the television technique of 'panning in'. For instance, one might see at the beginning of a film, the blue globe of the earth whirling in space. Then we pan in close enough to see towns and cities. Then we pan in near enough to see a particular town, then the streets, then the houses, a particular street, a house, a door etc. Then a man coming through the door and we see his clothes, his bag, and by the TV technique that enables us to see what is in things, we may see what is in the bag -- perhaps he's carrying a gun or perhaps it's only his sandwiches for lunch!

If you consider this quite useful means which enables us to focus our consciousness on where we are supposed to look, so that the story can develop, then we realise how it shows the limitations of our senses. If you were far off you couldn't see a man coming out of his house. Even if he is just a few hundred yards away you can't see him properly, and further than that you probably can't see him at all. Even a few hundred yards away you don't see things in detail. If you see someone walking down the road toward you, you can just see a figure, later you see it is a man, then a tall man with black hair or whatever he really looks like.

An object has to be within a certain range before it can be observed by ordinary eyes. We need telescopes or microscopes to get a thing into the range at which we can observe -- to make things bigger or bring them within range. To observe tiny particles -- bacteria, protons and photons -- we need optical aids. Of course we take all of this for granted. But if we really consider what the senses are, we realise that unaided by optical instruments or devices like televisions, we're not able to use anything like the whole range of what the eye can actually see.

The eye also can only see what it is conditioned to see. Primitive people can't see photographs for instance. They will take a photograph and turn it upside down and look at the back of it and be unable to realise that it is a picture of a group of people or of themselves.

Captain Cook, who discovered Tasmania, had an interesting note in his diary about this question of what the eye is accustomed or conditioned to see. He left his sailing ship out in the bay and got into a small boat and rowed with a few men up to a beach. Some people came to meet him, Aborigines, very friendly and very willing to know him. Of course they had no common language but they managed to communicate by signs and the natives indicated that they wanted to know, 'where did you come from?' They saw of course that he and his men had come in a little boat and that he rowed up onto the shore. But they realised that he hadn't come from a nearby island or anywhere that they knew. Captain Cook indicated, lying out in the bay, the large ship, with sails furled. The Aborigines could not see it at all. They could not see anything there, because they knew nothing at all about great big sailing ships. Their eyes were not accustomed or conditioned to see something that they didn't know about at all. They could see the small rowing boat because they knew about small rowing boats but they could not see the sailing ship, which must of course have looked quite small because of the distance.

When considering what we are conditioned to see, it's interesting to think what happens to a person who has been blind since birth and who recovers sight for the first time. One might believe that he/she could suddenly see everything, and what a beautiful world it is. But they can see nothing -- just a jumble of images, of colour and movement. They don't know how near or how far away everything is. They don't know the shape of anything; where one thing is relative to another; or the texture or type of thing they are looking at.

So the formerly blind man, struggling to get accustomed to using sight must, of necessity shut his eyes in order to 'see' his way to walk across the room. If he walks with his eyes open he will bump into everything and fall over. If an orange is put down in front of him on the table and he is asked 'what do you think that is?' he has no idea how big it is, what its shape is, what its colour is or what its texture might be. But let him touch it and hold it in his hand, and he will say 'that's an orange!' He is not conditioned to use his eyes and so he needs to learn from the beginning. I remember one rather sad story about a man who recovered sight in this way, and was so completely defeated by his inability to use it, that he took to walking around with his eyes closed, never looking at anything. He couldn't make the enormous effort to use the wonderful attribute of sight.

Hearing. We can only hear within a certain range of sounds, just as we can only see within a certain range of size and distance. Sound of course, is caused by vibrations: heavy throbbing vibrations in the lower ranges or very light and very rapid ones higher up the scale. Some people can't hear very high notes at all. Only some people can hear the cry of a bat, on Summer evenings.

A dog can hear a supersonic whistle which we can't hear. Dogs can hear a range of sounds much higher than we can. The vibrations are too fine for our ears. In the lower ranges, dogs and animals seem as though they may have the ability to experience the heavier vibrations. We know that dogs and cats become uneasy when thunder is in the air, but this may be, that there is a heavy feeling in the air. But those who are old enough, will remember how uneasy dogs and cats used to get in air raids before the air raid siren sounded. They would begin to prowl up and down. The assumption must be that they could hear aircraft taking off or approaching when they were not even in the reach of the Radar. My own two cats will often tell me when somebody enters my cottage garden and comes along the path towards the front door. They raise their heads and swivel their radar-like ears towards the hall. Bossy Boots rather likes visitors and will come with me if he sees I am going to the door. Pussy Willow settles down to sleep again as soon as she knows she has alerted me to the fact that there is someone there!

We ourselves only hear a few octaves of sound. But sound does exist, in the form of vibrations both above and below the ranges that we can detect.

Smell, Touch and Taste. Its not quite as easy to speak of possible extensions to the other three senses, as to sight and hearing. We all know what it is to experiences different textures by touch -- rough or smooth etc. And we know about different smells, different tastes. Our five physical senses are limited. But we can sometimes experience super sensory perceptions, above and below the normal range. We need of course to go outside of the senses completely to experience what is known as extrasensory perception or ESP.

Supersensory Experience.

It's easier to speak of the super sensory aspects of taste, touch and smell, rather than their 'extended use.' Hearing and sight, have extended use and supersensory aspects as well.

Smell. Many people have the experience of smelling something that is not in the realm of ordinary scent, such as the scent of flowers or incense for instance when there are no flowers or incense in the room. It may be possible to get a scent that has no apparent physical cause at all. People may say 'I smell my Mother's perfume.' And yet Mother died long ago. Or 'my Father's tobacco'.

Enid Case, who lived in the West Country, experienced the scent of flowers, and particularly lilies, on one occasion when there were no flowers there. She was so interested in her experience that she wrote a letter to Good Housekeeping asking if anyone else had ever had such an experience. To her surprise many people answered her letter saying they had indeed, and giving many detailed occurrences.

Teilhard de Chardin said of these inexplicable scents: 'I have considered whether it may be something to do with the spiritualisation of matter. Whether in some way something within the room or the place where that person is was giving off the scent of its own spiritual nature. Enid Case wrote a book called *The Odour of Sanctity*. She felt that there was something possibly holy about the scents, particularly flowers and the scent of incense which she became very conscious of. This has become a little classic on this subject of inexplicable scents and perfume.

When I was working with the Indonesian mystic Pak Subuh I experienced these super sensory perfumes, as did many others. We used to meet in the Royal Ballet School rehearsal rooms in Hammersmith, London. Every time I entered that large building I would get a very strong scent of incense as I entered and walked along a corridor. In fact, I was quite sure that incense was being burned habitually somewhere there. Then I discovered, after talking with people, that some other people could smell incense and others never did smell it; some people smelt it on certain evenings and not on others.

I discovered also that people had experiences of different scents. One lady said she always smelt rose otto, a very strong essential oil that comes from Bulgaria. Somebody smelt her Mother's perfume, which was Coty L'Aimant. Sometimes a lot of people would smell the incense or flowers, and people who had not smelt it at one time, would smell it on another occasion. There seemed to be a real scent, but not picked up by the ordinary narrow range of senses. Of course, ordinary scents are experienced by the little hairs in our noses being triggered off as we breathe in. They are made to move and vibrate a little by the vibration of the scent. But it almost seems as though these supersensory scents don't come by the nostrils They come beyond the realm of the ordinary.

During this time, my husband and I were living in an old house in Kent. On one occasion, our nine year old daughter said to me 'I can smell a wonderful smell coming from the cupboard under the stairs.' She was sniffing about and said 'it smells like incense.' Now she was normally at boarding school and I had not told her anything about Subuh, and I would not probably have discussed it with her as she was so young.. On that occasion I could smell nothing at all and yet I felt undoubtedly that it was something being triggered off by what I had been doing each day -- practising the Latihan, the Subuh spiritual practice. Occasionally people do get unpleasant experiences. I remember a medium, for instance, who used to complain that she got 'nasty smells' when she was doing her clairvoyant readings. I think, perhaps one wonders what entity may have been involved there! Perhaps purity of intent was lacking. One can't be sure. But in most cases supersensory experiences tend to be pleasant..

Touch. Sometimes people seem to feel touches that are beyond the realm of the ordinary senses: something like the arms or the face 'being touched as if by angel wings' somebody said to me. Or a movement in the air when there is no draught, no door or window is open and there is no actual movement. Some people have had a sense of somebody tapping them on the shoulder or stroking their forehead or smoothing their hair. I remember one person who felt she had been thumped on the back for no apparent reason! But more often this type of sense of touch is a light presence, perhaps like the touch of a gone beloved one.

Taste. Something may be tasted in the mouth, when it is not actually there. With the Maharishi Mahesh Yogi, when we were doing the TM (transcendental meditation) sometimes people experienced within their mouth what they thought was a beautiful pure taste as of spring water from a source high up in the mountains. I do remember one person who used to do the Latihan however, who used to taste and smell bacon and eggs! She was a rather large lady who clearly thought a great deal about her food. This started up in my mind the inner consideration of whether one tends to smell or taste what one wants. Perhaps really she wanted bacon and eggs, or perhaps she wanted spiritual food. Most of us appeared to be wanting spiritual experiences of one kind or another. We wanted to go higher.

Taste is mentioned in some of the ancient myths and legends, particularly the legends of King Arthur and the Knights of the Round Table. In Mallory's 'Morte D'Arthur' we are told that the Holy Grail, which of course is a vessel, a container, a chalice, is borne through the Hall by the Grail Maidens to where the knights are 'sitting at meat'. Everybody stops eating and they listen and they look and at once the Hall is filled with 'most sweet odours, most sweet savours'. And when they begin to eat again they all taste the most wonderful food that they have ever tasted. Each man has the food that he most desires. There is certainly an old tradition which indicates that the senses can be triggered off at this higher level. It is still in the range of the physical, but at a higher, more subtle, level of experience. It is supersensory.

Extrasensory Experience

Extrasensory perceptions are different from supersensory perception. Channelling is certainly beyond the physical senses. Voices heard *inside* oneself as distinct from received by the ears from an outer source, are surely beyond the five basic senses, and come into the range of ESP. To make full use of the senses is very important. But we possibly do need to go beyond them. We may go beyond by chance or perhaps by effort. We need to make full use of the possibilities of this body's fleshly form. The Spirit may manifest itself via the senses in the first instance. So any supersensory or extrasensory perceptions are very important.

With honesty of purpose and straightforward cleanness of intent, I think it is generally interesting or pleasing things that are experienced. If people experience anything unpleasant, it may be that they have dabbled in what are known as the 'black arts': perhaps trying to get power. It's no good to go for power for its own sake. Power comes as a side effect of going for a greater goal. It's no use to go for power for oneself. People who have that as their aim generally don't become very nice people. Often they seem to become gradually degenerate and very unhappy.

Attempts to develop supersensory experience are seen even in the Bible. In the Old Testament the Jews were told how to make incense; what herbs and oils are to be used for an incense for praise or for mourning or for rejoicing. Making something to reproduce at an ordinary sensory level that which is essentially of the Spirit is inherent in this idea. Incense rises up, starts one on the path, like a tool of the Spirit: just as a microscope or telescope or a microphone, are tools of the body.

The first tools are always tools for the body. Man dug with his hands before he realised that he could make a stone or piece of wood into a spade. Then he made a proper spade. We are quite at liberty to invent tools, whatever tools will help us along the way. If we get a scent that isn't there, we get something of a supersensory nature. If we burn incense we are imitating the real thing, trying to reproduce the odour of sanctity to put us in the right state for our work, our meditation etc. When ESP starts it can often be via the super sensory, as we become more aware. It is as though we each have a radio receiver which is picking up bits and pieces of a wonderful symphony orchestra, but we are not sensitive to half the notes. Of course music too is a tool to recreate other worlds, via the sense of hearing. Within the realms of the octaves which we hear, octave upon octave can be triggered off.

Observation is a means. The senses are the media. And beyond the normal ranges are the supersensory ranges and beyond that extrasensory experiences.

If you hear a sound or a voice, not emanating from outside but seeming inside yourself, giving a message or saying something, then your mind gets engaged at once and asks 'what is this?' If something of significance is heard, one's mind takes a leap forward perceiving the meaning for one's self. Then one may possibly be within the realms of ESP.

This is what one hopes for if one is experimenting with channelling as suggested in the last chapter. A lot of time nothing much happens. But occasionally there may be something interesting. We want to know, what is this voice? Is it recognisable? What does it say? Of course 'hearing voices' is very much on the edge of what is permissible to normal minds. People who are schizophrenic or mentally abnormal in some way, do frequently hear voices telling them to do this or do that. So the intellect must be engaged, if one hears a voice. One must be in command of oneself. I don't think it's a very good idea to actually court voices as it were. But never the less one may sometimes hear something which is interesting. Then, not to be afraid, but to ponder on what you have heard, and whether it increases your knowledge or understanding is worth doing.

Making Spiritual Tools

Basically we have the five senses: the supersensory perception which is outside the range of our ordinary every day experience; the ESP when something comes in which is beyond the senses altogether. ESP includes an enormous range of possible experiences other than hearing voices. The five senses are our tools for working in this world. The super senses are like a honed tool for finer and finer work. If we can grasp and use them with our mind, then it is like learning to make a new tool and using it for higher work. So the making of tools is part of a growth of consciousness. From the hands to the spade, to the horse drawn plough, to the huge mechanical diggers of today, man has developed his tools for wordly use. We are now looking for tools for spiritual use.

To fashion anything we need tools, so we need to think ahead about the spiritual tools that we have inherited from our forbears. The Tree of Life of the Kabbalah; the Horoscope chart and the whole of the practice of Astrology; the Major Arcana of the Tarot cards and so on. And we can see all these traditional methods of getting inner knowledge as tools for development of understanding. We can also consider methods of divination: tarot, the runes, crystals, scrying, sand reading, tassiography (reading the tea leaves), and so on. The diagrammatic tools and divinatory tools are the ones which should interest us if we want to learn and make full use of the possibilities of our bodies, our minds and the spirit which lives within us. So we shall discuss them in greater detail later in this book.

Suggested Exercises

It can be very helpful to do experiments with the senses and here are two that you could well try.

1. Each one of us has around us an energy field. Become aware of other people's energy fields by testing in this way. Find a helpful friend. Stand a little more than arm's length away from him/her. Stand with your hands palm outwards, near your own shoulders. Begin to put your hands forward, until you encounter a slight resistance. Most people have an energy field of about two or three feet around themselves. Those who are very strong and motivated, often have an

energy field which can be quite easily detected. You need to move your hands very slowly forward because the resistance you encounter is only very slight but it can be detected.

Being conscious of the energy fields around living things gives one a considerable advantage. It also explains why we instinctively shear off from being too close to strangers. We usually don't like to sit crammed up against somebody in a train or on a bus for instance and we instinctively try to move away a little. This is because our energy field is overlapping other energy fields. We only really want to be in the energy field of those who are close and dear to us. It can be quite uncomfortable to impinge on somebody else's energy field or to feel them impinging on ones own.

It's interesting to realise that people with a strong energy field generally don't get mugged! The intending mugger for some reason will shear off. He will not try to penetrate a strong energy field of a confident person. People who go to self-defence groups are taught something like this. To experiment and become aware of the energy field round the people near you but particularly with strangers in shops, restaurants and so on is an interesting and worthwhile experiment.

2. Observe other people, in a train or a restaurant for instance. Be discreet! Don't stare at them too intently or they will sense it and become uncomfortable. Look with your ordinary senses and observe very clearly the type of person, what they look like, their age, their colouring, what they are wearing, what their body language suggests to you. When you have really looked and used all your senses to observe with your ordinary eyes, draw back into yourself a little. Close your eyes for a moment. Then opening your eyes and letting them go slightly out of focus, see if you can observe with your inner eye what appears to be with or behind that person. You are seeing with the senses but not with the ordinary senses. You might pick up something like an apparent mother figure or a partner or a house or a place or a beloved animal that

seems to accompany that person or something from their own childhood. It is via the senses that you do this, but not the ordinary senses. If you get very adept at this you can sit in a train on a long journey and at the end of the journey you will know a great deal about all your fellow passengers! Of course you will never be able to prove what you know unless you get into conversation with anyone but you may have a sense of inner knowing.

This is a first step towards developing clairvoyance. It comes first via the observations, via the ordinary senses, then by super sensory perception and occasionally indeed extrasensory perception may be triggered off by this means.

If you seriously try these experiments you will probably be surprised to find what you can experience. You are well on the way to developing your self towards higher consciousness.

7

To Sleep Perchance To Dream

We have been talking about the five basic senses: sight, hearing, taste, touch and smell and their possible usage in normal waking life. But we spend between a quarter and a third of our life asleep. What then happens to the senses?

All forms of life appear to have this need to withdraw from conscious awareness of the outer world for some hours out of every twenty four. And of course some animals hibernate -- withdrawing into sleep and a very low metabolic level for the winter months every year. During sleep the heart beats more slowly, the energy output is negligible and all functions operate at a much lower level than during wakefulness. The body and the mind both appear to need these periods to refresh themselves and recover from the experiences of normal living in the world.

In sleep we appear to be neither wholly in nor wholly out of the normal world. It is a very curious aspect of our lives that we have to retreat into this: and that deprivation of the sleeping period becomes increasingly uncomfortable until it results in a total loss of consciousness into a deep sleep which can't be resisted. In sleep the mind is free to wander into dreams.

However, in sleep we are obviously still here in our bodies, and examining the sleep state can be very interesting indeed. Our dream world has a certain reality of its own.

Scientific experiments show that dreaming takes place only during certain periods of sleep: the periods known as R.E.M. (Rapid Eye Movement). These seem to occur at intervals during the night and possibly more markedly just before waking. Of course they have been much tested and examined without anyone being able to come to a clear conclusion as to what dreaming actually is.

Apart from the deep dreaming state when all sorts of strange things seem to be happening in our minds, there are also some semi-dream states. They are called the hypnogogic and hypnopompic states. They are very important in understanding what sleep may be.

Hypnogogia is when we are falling asleep and hypnopompia as we are just coming out into full waking. During this period, we half know what is going on but we are not consciously in control of our mind's activities. These two states have also been much investigated. The scientist Timothy Leary is probably better known for his experiments with LSD in the 1960s, than for other aspects of his studies. But he did a lot of work on dreams. He wrote 'the hazy areas on the border between sleep and wakefulness are of a special interest to scientists. They are threshold states between being fully awake and fully asleep. They have aroused a special interest because of their similarity to meditative and trance states. Some people think that meditators and practitioners of various types of trance states have learnt to maintain hypnogogia without falling asleep. Others disagree. Some believe that meditators may get into a higher state of consciousness and that hypnogogia is simply a door way to these higher states.'

Hypnogogia is much easier for most people to observe than hypnopompia. We are all conscious of being in that half and half state when we are saying to ourselves 'I am going to sleep. In a few minutes I shall be asleep,' and our mind begins to wander illogically. It has temporarily lost its normal waking rationality. The hypnopompic state is often curtailed by us, because when we wake up we very often have to get up quickly. So we banish it. But on lazy occasions such as on holiday or Sunday mornings, when we don't have to get up, some of us may luxuriate in the experience of the hypnopompic state. We are saying to ourselves 'I am awake but I don't have to get up yet' and allowing our mind to range as it will. During this time we probably get unexpected versions of events, unexpected pictures, sounds, voices, messages, scraps of conversation, places never seen in actual life. They're coming from somewhere! But we don't know where.

If you have experimented with an attempt to establish a relationship with a guide, you may have experienced this half and half state when you make a vessel, attempt to become that vessel, make your invocation, and then wait. Your mind ranges doesn't it? You try to feel the presence of somebody and you seem to half go to sleep. Of course, if you have practised TM, (Transcendental Meditation), or any other form of deep meditation, you will be well aware that you can hear or be conscious of sounds going on in the room or in the world outside. And yet you appear not to be part of that world. You are neither asleep nor awake and you are almost in a trance. Of course a trance can normally be broken at will just by opening your eyes and stopping your meditation. There is a great similarity here to the natural states of entering sleep at night and leaving it in the morning.

The Hypnogogic State

Examining the hypnogogic state can show something quite interesting about the nature of your own mind. If you relax and let your mind wander, your thought generally picks up one thing after another in a kind of progression. Each thought triggers off another little thought and so on. But in hypnogogia, there is a strange lack of logicality. Things present themselves without any apparent order or linking. It's worth observing this state. But that doesn't mean yanking yourself back and out of well deserved sleep each night! Just try to observe and go on into sleep.

By allowing yourself to think during the experience: 'What

is this? What am I observing? What am I hearing? Where does it come from?' You can realise that you are in a realm outside ordinary every day material consciousness. You can let it go on, while becoming aware of it. You may ask yourself 'What is it bringing out? Am I bringing up things that I subconsciously know about my own self, about my past, or are they things happening somewhere else, to somebody else? What are these views, these mountain ranges I have never seen, this town where I have never been?' It's perfectly possible to be aware and examine these things with that part of your mind which is still conscious while at the same time allowing hypnogogia to continue until it falls away naturally as you go into sleep.

Observing hypnogogia and hypnopompia or the dream state, is not of course easy, because we lose them almost at once when we come into full wakefulness. Those who have tried writing down their dreams, know that although you may wake with a vivid dream in your mind and think you will write it in a moment, if you delay even long enough to get up and go to the bathroom, let alone make a cup of tea, it will be gone by the time you get back into bed and reach for your paper and pen. So if you are going to observe at all, you will need to be very stern with yourself. Keep a writing pad and pen beside your bed, and the minute you wake, grope for it and start to write down what is in your mind then. If you don't do so you will be amazed to realise how very quickly it passes beyond recall.

In the state of hypnosis -- and of course both these states are of a hypnotic type -- the mind is not activated by reason or accumulated experience. Everything has a strange kind of reality, and yet it's not quite real. It's worth experiencing all this consciously if possible.

The whole question of what dreams really are is very interesting. It has been much investigated of course but so much still remains to be learnt. What is the dream world? What is reality? Sometimes in life itself you may think 'am I dreaming? Is this it?' There are periods when people find that they can't seem to yank themselves out of a state of unreality or semi dreaming even though they are actually awake. There are many states between that state of extreme alert wakefulness, and a half awake state, and a dream state, when you have no idea what is coming next.

We have all sometimes said something like 'I could hardly believe it! I thought I was dreaming'. We mean something has happened in ordinary life with the illogicality we associate only with the dream world.

What is Reality?

If you get into the habit of observing your dream life, and in particular the hypnogogic and hypnopompic states, where you are already half conscious of being neither awake nor asleep, you may begin to realise how very unsure we are, if we are honest with ourselves, about what reality actually is. You remember Hamlet's speech 'To be or not to be' has in it the words 'to sleep perchance to dream. Aye, there's the rub.' Hamlet realises that he doesn't know, in the middle of all his troubles, what is reality. If he were to make an end of it, maybe there would be a worse reality to be faced. Or maybe just the same thing all over again. So what is waking? What is sleeping? What is the dream world? It's well worth thinking about this.

There is also another interesting practice that you may like to try. Its harder to do than just observing hypnogogia, or writing down dreams. This is the practice of 'lucid dreaming' This was first spoken about by Georges du Maurier, a Victorian novelist from that family from whom Daphne du Maurier was descended. He wrote a best selling book called *Peter Ibbotson,* much read and discussed in its own time though pretty well forgotten now. This had in it the words 'to dream true'.

Peter Ibbotson had the idea that if he could control his wild dreams, he would in some way be able to control his own destiny. But this would mean sleeping so lightly that he would know when he was asleep, and could order what he desired in the way of a dream life. .

Indian traditions suggest that it is not at all a good idea to 'sleep like a log'. The body and the mind don't need this heavy sleep, which we in the West are often rather proud to have experienced. It's said to be better if we sleep more lightly. The Maharishi Mahesh Yogi told me: 'You should always be aware you are asleep.' In hypnogogia/hypnopompia you are aware. It is part of the idea of developed man, that one knows when one is sleeping and when one is waking.

Lucid dreaming in theory means being able to control our life and our destiny. You learn more about the different parts of your mind. If you have a dream, especially if it is a nasty one, you can say to yourself: 'this is a dream. I don't want this.' You can change it. In ordinary life we are stuck with what is going on. But our dream lives need not control us to that extent. We all know the kind of nightmarish dream which we don't want at all and how we half wake ourselves up in an attempt to get rid of it saying 'it's only a dream.'

The idea of lucid dreaming would be to take this ability into the realms of ordinary fantastic dreaming -- the wildness and illogicality of the scenes and events that present themselves -- and make them into something more profitable. Perhaps by this means we can ultimately find ourselves more in control of life. A situation faced in a dream may ultimately be faced in life itself; or one may see the dream as being symbolic of something and one can learn something about one's own life through it. In lucid dreaming one should be consciously aware of dreaming and the rational mind can then take control of the dream.

This gives a great possibility of problem solving. It's very much the custom when people are faced with a problem to say 'I won't decide now. I'll sleep on it.' And of course this is exactly the idea of getting access to those deeper parts of the mind which enable one to understand more profoundly the roots of our problems and so to solve them.

Lucid Dreaming

'Doing this should save an awful lot of psycho analysis!' said Timothy Leary. The whole idea is to improve the access to our own subconscious mind, or indeed our higher selves. We may learn to understand ourselves by this means. It gives great scope for self investigation of psychological problems, perhaps taking us back into our early childhood, or perhaps even into previous lives.

If you could go consciously into the hypnogogic state with a problem in mind, seeking to understand it fully and to solve it; and then go on into sleep and into a lucid dream state, it can well be that you will surmount many of the difficulties of your ordinary life. You could get a much clearer view of why you find yourself in certain situations and why you behave in the manner that you do. If you have relationship problems for instance, or job problems, you can get the low-down on them by this means.

You can order your dreams almost in the same way as you might look for a guide. You can say to yourself 'this is what I want' and work towards the idea of drawing from your own higher self, perhaps via a guide. You might mentally arrange to meet a wise old soul or some appropriate archetype, to show you what is causing a health problem for instance, or some other particular difficulties that you don't know how to deal with in the ordinary way. A difficult decision that may be clouded with emotions will sometimes reveal itself in a different light. The subconscious or higher mind may have the answers all the time, if we can only improve our access to it. There are so many experiences and discoveries which become possible, once lucid dreaming is mastered, and there are many therapeutic benefits.

To this extent it clearly doesn't matter, as Catherine Rydell said, if one's guide is a figment of one's imagination or a separate entity or an aspect of one's higher self or a previous incarnation. It is the aspect of the encounter that matters.

'We need to find methods of recognising the dream state

and of maintaining awareness throughout the dream,' Leary says. It's easy to become engrossed in the dream and to lose lucidity. In those experiences of lucid dreaming we have the difficulty of maintaining lucidity. And there's also the problem of avoiding waking up because of the excitement of recognising that you are dreaming! 'It takes some long term practice to get the knack of attempting and maintaining lucid dreaming.'

Of course we can't know for sure whether reality is here and now or somewhere else; or whether we're dreaming all the time. We can get into very deep water over this one, but the more we think of it, the more we come to realise whether a dream is just a dream or whether one is in some way in control of it.

An acquaintance of mine, Lou Sutton, who made a study of dreams, once wrote to me 'if you think you are half awake and you're not sure if you are dreaming or whether it is real, there are tricks for finding out. E.g. if you think you are in a room and you switch on a light and it doesn't come on, its a dream. If you look out of your kitchen window and the view is all wrong, it is a dream. Use this, and also observe the waking state, to say to yourself 'am I dreaming or is this real?' so that in actual dreaming you will be able to differentiate between that fairly useless state where one is at the mercy of everything. And that 'something' which will lead us to be in command of our own destiny.'

CatalepticTrance

There is another interesting state which some people experience, and that is waking up and being unable to move one's body or even feeling one is unable to wake up. This is a state of cataleptic trance. It seems to be an indication that while one is half awake, parts of the mind are still not functioning normally. You may wake and feel that you can't move your hands or your feet or your legs or arms.

Sometimes children experience this. And some people experience it once or twice in a lifetime and are often very frightened by it.

The interesting thing about this is that a state of cataleptic trance can very easily occur in practitioners of deep meditation, if they are not properly supervised by a real master or qualified teacher. I remember it occurring at a gathering in the mountains with an Indian master, where people, having been helped to go deeply into meditation, found that they couldn't arouse themselves. They would be conscious of sitting or lying and hearing talking going on around them, and knowing what was going on, but couldn't bring themselves back into full consciousness. Indian masters have ways of arousing a student in this state by passing a hand in a circular motion lightly above the head of the hypnotised one and calling his or her name softly. They will slowly come out of it. Where there is no qualified person able to deal with a situation like this there may be an attempt to arouse the person by force, shaking them or speaking loudly to them. This has very obvious dangers from a psychic point of view.

I remember one man who got into this state, alone in his bedroom in a hotel, on this meditation course. He was terrified, by being unable to snap out of it. Ultimately, apparently, he fell into a deep sleep. He woke up later able to move freely, but he was so frightened by the experience that he packed his bags and went home very quickly! This cataleptic trance state, which can take the form of not being able to move, also has with it the fringe experiences of knowing you are asleep and not being able to wake up. Or alternatively thinking repeatedly that you have got up, that you are awake and that you have got up and got dressed, that you have started out on your day's work, only to realise that in fact you are still asleep in bed. These things are part of ordinary living and may be experienced particularly in times of fatigue or stress. They occur rarely. They're not normally a source of great concern. But meditation practices which induce such experiences, either on purpose or by chance, are obviously highly dangerous and in my opinion shouldn't be dabbled with.

Another very interesting aspect of the dream life is the question of the time element in dreams. There was a very interesting book written in about 1925 by John Dunne who was extremely interested in dreams and in particular by the fact that his own dreams seemed to reflect in some way his own past or his own future. Sometimes he thought that the dreams he had were symbolic of something in his mind at the time of dreaming or of something that was about to happen.

An Experiment with Time

Dunne set himself to observe and to write down in great detail every dream that he had and ultimately wrote a most interesting volume called *An Experiment with Time*, which became a bit of a classic and I believe is still in print. He discovered that the mind appears to range a few days back or forth within the dream state, reflecting often quite mundane things in his life. Of course, the ones that had already occurred were not so interesting, although if they came in a strange version that was recognisable but not quite like the actual event, they were interesting for that reason alone. But when something happened in a dream and later on happened in his life, then it was much more interesting. It suggested to him something about the nature of time. He thought that time has no reality itself, but could be proved to have certain limited parameters within which it manifests itself.

He produced many examples of the kind of dreams in which the mind ranged forward and picked up something which was later reproduced in a slightly different version. One example was a recollection of having dreamt that he was going along Piccadilly when he saw a large umbrella standing on the pavement outside the Piccadilly Hotel. The ferrule was upwards and the umbrella itself was standing on its own stick, which had no handle or hook on it, just a straight stick. He noted this down, because at that time he was writing down every detail of what he dreamt each night. A few days later he was on the top of a bus, travelling down Piccadilly. When he looked down he saw, what we should probably nowadays describe as, 'an old bag lady' stumping along Piccadilly carrying an identical umbrella in her hand, holding it by the ferrule and putting the stick, which had no handle, on the ground as though it were a walking stick. This trivial incident, apparently meaning nothing, nevertheless had the implication of a mind ranging almost at random outside time and picking up bits of an actual event, which was yet to occur.

I myself experimented in this way for quite a long time and found it very intriguing. I made a record of a number of different experiences. One I remember particularly. I dreamt of a wellington boot lying by itself in the snow. The following morning I read in the local newspaper a sad story of an old country woman who had gone down to feed her chickens in the snow and had slipped and fallen and broken her hip. In an attempt to attract attention, as her cries were evidently not heard, she had taken off one of her wellies and tossed it up the path towards the gate hoping that someone would see it and realise something was wrong. Unfortunately nobody did so and the poor soul died by herself of hypothermia and was found much later. The curiosity about this dream from my point of view, was that I had not picked up anything of the anguish, the pain, the fear experienced by a woman dying in the snow. I had simply 'picked up' the wellington boot. I could not, of course, have done anything whatsoever about my dream even if I had wakened up at that point. I could not have known it was a reflection of something actually occurring around the time, or in advance of, when I had dreamt it. I could not have known the significance of the boot in the snow, or where it was or who it belonged to. The old woman was completely unknown to me. But somehow my half-asleep mind had ranged and honed in on it. Perhaps a more advanced person would have recognised it was a cry for help, and where its owner lay. It gave me a great deal of food for thought at the time.

Experimenting by observing one's dreams in this way takes time and patience, but to do so is very rewarding. It does throw much greater light on the nature of the body, the mind and the Spirit, which make up our threefold being in his world in which we live.

Suggested Exercises

1. Observe and write down your dreams for at least a week.

2. Observe the hypnogogic (going into sleep) state and the hypnopompic (waking up in the morning) state and see how you can watch yourself going to sleep and waking up. Notice the difference between thinking in that state and thinking when fully awake.

3. Attempt lucid dreaming by going to sleep with a thought in your mind that you will dream of some particular thing, perhaps some problem that you hope to solve. See whether anything comes of it.

4. As you go about your day to day affairs ask yourself at intervals 'Is this reality?'

8

Pathways of the Ancients

Perhaps the Earth also dreams, imagining throwing up flowers and dreaming of perpetual fecundity; only to awaken to floods or the aridity of deserts, or the effects of the predatory hand of man.

But the Earth has its energy fields the same as we do ourselves and in co-operating with them, learning to recognise and use them, we may be sharing in an ancient eternal dream of the universe.

Early man would seem to have had considerable knowledge of how to use the powers within the Earth itself. Leylines and standing stones are evidence of this.

The word leyline was first used by Alfred Watkins (born 1855). He toured Herefordshire with his father who was a brewer. He had to go back and forth on horse back or with horse and cart over a number of years from boyhood onwards. He was evidently a little psychic. He began to notice strange alignments in the countryside; ancient beacons, marker stones, all seeming to follow straight lines. He saw this especially when studying a map. He realised that churches often lie in a straight line and he thought they might follow ancient man-made track ways. He marked fifty one churches on a map of one area that he was in, and found that in eight instances there were four churches which fell into a clear line and, in one case, even five churches. He thought this might be just chance so he took a piece of paper and marked fifty one crosses at random, to test this theory. When he put his ruler through them, as he had put his ruler through the map of churches, he found that this random marking gave only one line of as many as four, and none at all of five. So he thought that the churches must be in a line more than just by chance.

As the years passed Watkins tramped the country side with a few friends looking for confirmation of his idea that churches, ancient monuments, dolman stones, megaliths, fell in lines. In some cases he found eight or nine. Then one day when he was quite old and he was sitting on a rock somewhere in the country side and looking at a map, and out at the country and down to the map on his lap, he had a strange psychic experience. He seemed to see a web of vein-like lines criss-crossing the map from hill top to hill top. Churches and castles, mounds and moats, holy wells and ancient cross roads, were on the lines, showing as if this was how it was many years ago. He began to give lectures on this subject and he wrote what is now the most classic book on the subject of early leyline hunting: *The Old Straight Track.*
In the years afterwards very much ley hunting followed, as other interested people began to research, following the ideas that Watkins had begun to develop. It gradually became evident that the lines were not by any means all old tracks, for they sometimes went over hilltops and across lakes, where people could never have walked.

It soon became evident that many of these lines led to stone circles and important prehistoric monuments and that angles of some sort made by stone markers might have astronomical or astrological significance. It seemed that some sort of natural lines, below the surface of the earth had been known to ancient man, and that ancient artifacts had been built by people who were far from being primitives.

The Michael Line

In 1973 John Michell published his work on what became known at that time as the Glastonbury to Avebury leyline. This was later discovered to extend from St Michael's Mount, off the coast of Cornwall, via Glastonbury and Avebury. And then on to Bury St Edmunds -- a distance of 380 miles -- and then up to the little village of Hopton, in Norfolk, where it appears to go out to an old ruined church very near the shore and then possibly right out to sea. Later this became known as the Michael Line. A number of churches dedicated to St. Michael or St. Michael and All Angels are found on this line. Mitchell also found a Salisbury to Stonehenge line and he thought that this went right up to the Lake District. This became known as the Mary Line. Several churches dedicated to St. Mary the Virgin figure in ancient places on the Mary Line. So the idea that there were long lines across country became firmly established. The ancients knew them, and evidently the early Christians did too.

But let's look back to a near contemporary of Alfred Watkins. Guy Underwood (born in 1883) introduced a new concept to the "Old Straight Track" idea and carried the work further in a different way. His main book *The Pattern of the Past* is very detailed and much more authoritative than many that have followed afterwards by people who have not gone so deeply into these things.

Underwood became interested in dowsing in the village where he lived. He found that the old traditional water diviners, who looked for places to dig a well for instance, attached very much importance to the prehistoric standing stones. Water diviners are often strongly affected by standing stones and he thought that the stones might convey what he called earth energies -- subtle changes in the magnetic field of the earth which might be picked up by the stones: electromagnetism. He saw that the dowsers steered clear of the stones because they seemed to get what was almost like an electric shock.

If you approach one of the ancient stones with your hands extended, (in the way you may have done when looking for energy fields around your friends) you may find that there is a slight tingling as you get within the energy field of the stone. The ancient standing stones tend to have quartz in them, and quartz is a conductor of energy. Gradually, Underwood began to think that the people who had built the old monuments, and he was particularly interested in Stonehenge, the biggest of them all -- used the enormous upright stones with quartz in them to go down into the earth and up above, with the idea of conducting the energy of the earth and making it available to mankind. So standing stones may have been placed at gathering points or important places, or in particular at places of worship. They were the power points. They were said to be "the place where God dwells".

Professor Alexander Thom, in Oxford in the 1940s to 1960s, and Professor T. C. Lethbridge in Cambridge at about the same time, followed up a lot of Underwood's ideas and the even earlier ideas of Watkins. They became very interested in the stones and the trackways and the interlinking of monuments and markers, which seemed in some cases to show true astronomical angles and possibly extraordinary knowledge of mathematical and astronomical calculations.

They found that strong electromagnetic energy from the stones could be measured by a gaussometer, an instrument invented in the nineteenth century by Professor Gauss of Cambridge. The gaussometer was, I think, the forerunner of the sort of metal detector devices that people use today or that the water mains experts use to trace where their pipes are. They make a rapid clicking noise whenever they get near the site of whatever they are looking for, water or metal. Recently I watched a Water Board man searching between my cottage and the country road, to install a water meter. He needed to find the route the old underground pipe followed, for it was not an obvious route. It was interesting to me to watch him locate it. This job would have been done by a local water diviner, long ago.

It seemed apparent to Thom and Lethbridge that the isolated stones were never placed anywhere by chance and gradually the two men realised that a complex network could be found all over the world as well as just in England. There are many alignments in the Middle East, in that area of Iran and Iraq which is largely desert for instance, where ancient observatories stood on the alignments. Not crude observatories but beautifully calculated and angled to show the rising and the setting of the sun, the waxing and the waning of the moon and picking out different seasons of the year in the stars.

The Lunar Cults

Of course nobody has ever discovered exactly what were the beliefs or aims or ambitions of the people who built these ancient artifacts or indeed how they moved and erected the great stones. Many of the earliest ones seemed to belong to lunar cults. That is, the people who were interested in the waxing and waning of the moon and the position of the moon in the heavens, and its apparent effect on mankind.

In about 5000 BC, that is the time of the megalithic age and the period that Thom himself concentrated on, astronomically the angle of the Earth was a declination of twenty three and a half degrees i.e. the angle of the sun above the celestial equator, as measured from the Earth's centre. The power of the stones seemed to be magnified if they were laid out using this angle. This is quite a difficult angle to be able to measure but he was finding it everywhere as he began to measure the stone circles.

Then one day he realised that if he drew a rectangle nine inches long by four inches high, a diagonal line laid out across this would give the exact twenty three and half degree that the ancients were using -- a very easy measure in fact once you know how. So it seemed, that the forces of heaven and earth were linked by these early people. It would seem as though one affected the other and this was the basis of the angles at which many of the stones were placed.

Guy Underwood had begun to look for what he called "geodetic lines", and he went on to the age of eighty one, still measuring not only the stone circles, the angles and the exact placing of the stones, but how they were linked across country. He saw that the vast monuments were clearly not just placed at random. He taught himself to dowse -- the water diviners' craft. He began to find underground radiating springs which he called blind springs: i.e. they did not come right up to the surface. They seemed to rise perpendicularly from deep down in the earth and then to spread out into springs in several directions somewhere near the surface. He found that blind springs could always be found by dowsing at the centre of the ancient sites and therefore it was clear that these sites were placed according to geological considerations, as well as by the planets, the sun and the moon. He amassed an enormous amount of data on this. While he too considered that they might be to do with lunar cults or solar and lunar cults, he could only broadly say that he felt the placing of them was something to do with the wellbeing of man on this Earth.

Underwood found there were three types of lines, which he called water stats, aqua stats, and track lines. He labelled them all together as geodetic lines. All old roads and tracks do appear to be laid out on track lines which he found he could dowse along. He discovered that if there is an old road which is then diverted by a modern loop or diversion of some sort, the dowsing rod would lead him along the old way. Dowsing did not respond to the modern loops or diversions in any way and he thought this was very significant.. He found that aqua stats were very plentiful in the old religious spots such as Stonehenge and sometimes there were complex spirals and loops round the stones.

He thought that the force, generated in the earth, was probably a wave motion perpendicular to the Earth's surface and which had great penetrative power and affected the nerve cells of animals and humans -- which is how people can actually dowse. He found that spiral patterns involving mathematical laws and principles were everywhere, including the principle of three and seven and that these occurred a lot in the old churches. He found that ancient churches generally stood on the leylines. There was at least one blind spring under each church, and dowsing around them he came to the conclusion that the blind spring would generally rise where the altar was. There was sometimes also a power spot at the chancel step and another one at the font. He discovered this to be true in the large and ancient cathedrals as well as the small wayside churches. Of course in many cases churches were built on very ancient sites already thought to be holy and used by the Druids or by the early wandering Christian saints, who lived alone, and chose or located a power spot on which to settle.

Animal Trackways

Underwood agreed with Alfred Watkins that the earliest use of the leylines might have been as tracks Animals tend to use the old tracks. They walk them knowing somehow that it is the right way to go. Early man learnt to use them for the same purpose.

When I lived in the New Forest, I observed this with the forest ponies. Although they can roam freely, they tend to walk the same tracks and ways, generation after generation. If you observe the countryside from some little height, you can often see track ways in the turf which obviously go back for hundreds, possibly thousands of years. The sheep walk them, the cattle walk them, and wild animals such as foxes and badgers tend to run along those same ways as though impelled to keep to them. It is as if they were some sort of guidelines to take them to where they want to go.

The New Forest ponies seemed to be very sensitive to the right places to have their foals. I soon began to think that these were probably in the areas where the blind springs were. There would perhaps be a hollow with one or two small trees bending over it. The presence of the trees in what otherwise might be open moor-land would of course possibly indicate that there was water somewhere down there. I noticed that when a mare was about to foal she would tend to go to one of those places and into privacy under a tree. The rest of the herd would follow and be peacefully grazing around the area and not disturbing her. And then a few hours later she would emerge with her new-born tottering foal coming with her, and the whole herd would move on.

I also observed places where a fox for instance, would come to a ditch and a hole in the hedge. Then cross a field at an angle and come out through another ditch and hole and away across the country side, and one could see that the animal had used that track for a very long time indeed. Clearly animals do know about geodetic lines and do know about the power points.

There is another strange allied mystery in the elephants graveyards in Africa. It has been observed that when an old elephant is about to die, the herd will often conduct it, pushing and helping and accompanying it to the place where it is the right place to die, and where other elephants have previously died. As the elephant lies down her fellow elephants will stand around sometimes touching or stroking with their trunks. When the death is over, they will move away and leave him or her there. So somehow they seem to know the right place to go, where the animal's body will be received back by the earth, and the spirit, whatever it may be, will go free.

The Knowledge of the Freemasons

There is an ancient tradition that churches and cathedrals were frequently laid out according to plans given by the Freemasons. If monks or priest and people wanted a church built, they would send for the Freemasons, who were a wandering band like an early trade union. These masons would not admit to the bondage of a particular master, probably because they knew far more than the boss who might employ them! The monks or people told the Freemasons more or less where they wanted the church, and they would then align it by dowsing and finding the blind springs, the power spots, saying exactly how to place it and making the basic plan.

Churches are by tradition built from East to West (the altar being at the East end). But they are sometimes not exactly aligned according to the compass. This seems to be because it was necessary to align them slightly off the true compass point in order to take in the blind springs that were available at that point.

There is also something quite interesting about the placing of lych gates at entrances to churchyards. By tradition a lych gate, which had a little roof over it, was a place where the coffin was placed by the bearers, while waiting to go into the church. It was evidently important that it lay on a blind spring. So the entrance to the churchyard would be where there was a suitable blind spring and the lych gate would be placed there.

We can see this for ourselves if we look at old country churches. Often we may find that the entrance to the churchyard is in some rather peculiar place, not obviously straight from the road. One might think, perhaps the road went a different way when the church was built. But often if you consider where the entrance is, you will see that it may be very strangely placed indeed and sometimes rather awkwardly placed. But this was where the power was found to be, therefore this had to be the natural way to go in.

Because animals are so sensitive to geodetic lines, old field entrances frequently seem to be over the power spots that they tended to walk along. In some parts of the country, especially down in the West Country, there are still very ancient stone gate posts, supporting modern gates in some cases. Stone gate posts go very deep into the ground. They were placed to indicate this is the way in, and they were placed where the animals wanted naturally to go in and out of the field.

Also field boundaries often seem to run along geodetic lines and by tradition in early days it tended to be the village priests, in pre-Christian and possibly even early Christian times, who knew how to dowse or who understood something about the underground forces in the earth. Therefore if somebody pinched someone else's land, or moved his boundary a bit, it would be the early priest who would know where the boundary actually was by dowsing for it!

The old milestones along the roads seem to have been marker stones of ancient origin. Sadly, modern highway authorities often destroy them.

The Rollright Stones

Nowadays of course we can't walk freely through Stonehenge as people used to be able to do when I was young. But we can still go to the smaller circles like the Rollright stones in the Cotswolds which is still open and simply looked after by one guardian person on duty. If you are reasonably sensitive, you will probably feel that there is indeed power there within the stones and within the circle itself. Even without a dowsing rod you may feel something beneath your feet, or you may feel that there is a tingling in your hands as you approach and touch the stones. There's a tradition that people go there for healing and that certain stones will be useful for certain purposes; one will tend to relieve rheumatism, another eases intestinal troubles and so on.

When I was there last, an elderly woman crippled with arthritis, was being helped to reach her favourite stone, and stand leaning back against it. She told me: 'I come here once a year. It's a long journey, but it's worth it, because I get relief for months.'

Those who dowse confidently with a dowsing rod have found a very strong spiral circle from the centre out to the stones themselves. Clearly this is a very big power spot indeed.

The angles at which the ancient stones stand are of enormous importance -- something which unfortunately is not realised at all by official bodies who, with good intentions but lack of ancient knowledge, will often heave them up if they're standing at an odd angle! Recumbent stones were not on the whole fallen stones but markers of some kind and sometimes there is an interesting phenomenon in that they can hold water in a hollow. An excellent example of this, until comparatively recently, was a recumbent stone to the right of the Hele stone at Stonehenge which had a hollow in which there was always water even at the hottest and driest times of the year. There are a number of other stones like this particularly in Ireland where there are usually myths and legends attached to them. It is difficult to know how they can remain wet, even in a drought, but it would seem that the quartz in them conducts water above from a blind spring below and there is often thought to be something holy about them.

At Glendalough, in Ireland, there is a stone like this known as the Deer Stone. Local lore has it that a mother who had no milk for her baby prayed there that the Lord would give her milk and a mother deer came down and deposited her milk each day in the hollow stone for the baby. For this reason that stone is still revered. The water in the Deer Stone is always there and the strange thing is that if you dip your fingers into it lightly it is almost like dipping your fingers into a holy water stoup in a church. There's something very strange about it. But once when I was there on a hot summer day, some yobos on motor bikes were racketing around, and then, thankfully, roared off again. Half an hour later I was near the Deer Stone and went to dip my fingers in it as usual. As soon as I touched the water, I shot back I knew there was something wrong.. I experienced a revulsion and the instinctive knowledge that this was not the 'real thing.' I realised a moment later that one of the young troublemakers must have urinated in it. Because of the colour of the stone and the warm air there had been nothing to warn me in advance that this was not the usual pure water. This nasty little incident remained in my mind because of the way that the sensitive sense of touch had somehow alerted me instantaneously.

Unfortunately as far as Stonehenge goes, when the circle

was still open to everybody, people would tend to put their crisp packets or cigarette ends or cans into the hollow and because the authorities didn't like this they simply filled it all in with concrete. So the sanctity of the place has gone. If they had known what they were doing they could have put some form of a guard over it, but clearly they attached no importance to it. In the same way officials from the Ministry of Works and other authorities, have capped some of the stones with plastic to protect them from the weather. And filled in hollows, marks and what they thought to be cracks in the standing stones, under the impression that they were protecting them. They thus eliminated many ancient signs and symbols, which were probably of profound significance once.

The Angled Stones

Where stones stand at an angle they usually indicate something far off and the angle at which they were meant to stand can usually be seen. If they have been raised upright, and you look at the top, you see that the top has usually been cut across at an angle and that angle would have been horizontal to the ground. There are many stones like this up in the Western Highlands of Scotland and in many cases they have been heaved upright enormously high; even twelve feet high and possibly twelve feet beneath the ground as well. But of course they no longer serve any purpose. A lot of them would originally have been angled over to the west towards the Paps of Jura, an island off the west coast. Between the two twin peaks the sun would set at mid-summer.

I remember having an extraordinary hunch about these stones when I was quite a small child, although I couldn't justify my strong feelings then! When I was about thirteen I was taken to Stonehenge, which in those days was completely open. You just drove your car up onto the grass and stopped wherever you wanted to. But there were a few men from the Ministry of Works, pottering about there and digging up one of the stones and heaving it up. I can remember talking to them and then with the certainty and innocence of childhood saying: "But this isn't right! It shouldn't be upright, it should be lying the way it is. Please leave it alone." My Father became quite angry because I was talking in such a cheeky way to these good workmen who were doing what they were told. But I was almost screaming inwardly, as I was dragged away, because I had such a strong gut feeling that what was being done was wrong. Of course I couldn't justify my ideas at all. But years later when I read about all this, I realised why it was probably wrong to heave up that stone which had been standing at a very low angle indeed and try to make it into one of the standing upright stones.

The two main ley lines, which I have already mentioned, the Michael and Mary lines have about them another very interesting curiosity. They were given these names, because it was discovered, that on the line from St Michael's Mount, right through to Hopton, there are an enormous number of churches dedicated to St Michael. And, on the one going up to the Lake District an enormous number of churches dedicated to St Mary or Mary the Virgin. It is quite impossible to explain logically how this could come about. One just has the feeling that somebody knew something! Of course the Freemasons who started at about 600 AD and went on for about a thousand years, were indeed Christian and it is possible that the dedication of the churches came from something that they knew or passed on in esoteric knowledge. In their later activities the Masons also directed the building of mansions and the laying out of old gardens in England, again aligning them according to the powers under the earth.

But when we are speaking of Stonehenge and other prehistoric artefacts, we are recognising builders from several thousand years before Christ.

The Glastonbury Zodiac

The possible mapping out of huge Zodiac circles on the landscape is a more mystical and more tenuous subject. Most people probably know of the Glastonbury Zodiac, first discovered by a Mrs Maltwood, who found that what looked like a goat's head on the map tallied with a place called Goat Lane. Later she discovered, that an area which looked rather like a bull's head, Taurus the Bull, had within that area a Pub called The Bull. This awakened her interest and she satisfied herself over some years that there was a huge Zodiac in the earth around Glastonbury, which you can more or less see on a map. And also another one at Kingston Upon Thames (a little less convincing perhaps). This is altogether a more individual, imaginative idea: whether there are Zodiacs marked by boundary lines, old field lines, old tracks and so on. Maybe there are. A diagrammatic map of the Glastonbury Zodiac is pretty convincing!

When I was working with a group in Norfolk we decided to go dowsing. We went to Castle Acre with our dowsing rods and worked around the ruins of the mediaeval castle and then, at the other end of the village, around the ruins of the enormous priory. We were very interested to find the way the dowsing rods moved, quite vigorously and strongly in certain areas. But one very curious thing was that some members of our party reacted strongly at the castle and found nothing at the Priory and others had strong reactions at the priory and found nothing at the castle. We also seemed to get an indication of possible male and female, masculine and feminine or positive and negative lines. We thought that there was possibly a masculine line which ran up to the high altar of the priory, (the Christos) and the feminine line to the Lady Chapel, dedicated to the Madonna. Of course all this is a matter of opinion, and we were not seeking to prove anything. What we were simply seeking to do, was to experience for ourselves that which we had previously only read in books or heard in lectures. There's a great deal to be said for experiencing things for oneself! And one day in your ponderings, you may know the dream that the Earth itself dreams in the strange lunar light.

Suggested Exercises

1. Make yourself a dowsing rod. You can do this by cutting a forked twig, preferably from a hazel tree. Or alternatively, do what most people do nowadays: make yourself a pair of dowsing rods from metal coat hangers. Cut a coat hanger with pliers, so that you have one long arm and one short arm. You then have a piece that you can bend easily into an L-shaped right angled rod. You need two coat hangers to make your pair. Ideally slip a piece of garden cane over each of the short arms so that the rods can swing very easily in your hands.

Take one rod in each hand, and holding them out in front of you, just feel how the rods will swing, sometimes gently and sometimes quite strongly towards each other, or away from each other or both in one direction. You'll find that as you walk around your garden or any field or open country that you know, you will get strong reactions in some places and very little in another. By experimenting with this you realise that you really are picking up some sort of earth energies. I think, almost anybody can get a reaction in this way.

2. Have a look at a map and see whether you can spot at least three churches, which seem to make a straight line. Then it's a good idea to visit them. It's quite interesting to see which saint they are dedicated to, and also to dowse around the church-yard or within the church itself if nobody minds.

3. On holiday, visit any stone circles or isolated standing stones that you hear of. Dowse around them, feel them with your hands and see if you can pick up the energy arising from them. You may get a lot of very interesting experiences from trying these practical exercises.

9

The Magic of Number

The little grand daughter of a friend of mine was brought home from her nursery school in disgrace. She had refused to do what was asked of her in the simple arithmetic exercises. She had folded her arms mulishly and then begun to cry and would not be consoled. She had been told to hold two strips of cloth, one of which had buttons on and the other button holes, and button them together saying 'one, two, three, four' as she did it. She had previously refused to put beads into a box, counting them in threes, or to separate building blocks into 'sets' according to colour. The teacher said 'she appears to have learning difficulties.'

The grandmother took the child on her knee later and asked her why she had not done as she was asked. She was obviously perfectly capable of understanding what to do. The little girl looked up into her face and said: 'They're silly. They don't do anything.' She explained that buttons should obviously button up something and beads were for making a necklace and building blocks were for making a house. Far from not understanding, she had used her brain rather in advance of the other children. That child of vision should go far even though she does encounter problems in the early stages of her education!

I remember well my own difficulty in 'seeing the point' of arithmetic, geometry, algebra and trigonometry which were not taught very imaginatively at my school. It was so boring to calculate the time taken for a bath to fill at a certain speed, while the water ran out at another but lesser speed. Why couldn't they just put the plug in? I asked. If some of you may have had the same problems, I hope that this chapter on the magic of number may grip you and make you feel that after all something can be 'buttoned up' as a result of your efforts. Bear with me over this if you are one for whom maths was never a problem.

My brother in law Rodney Collin, the philosopher, wrote a study programme not long before he died. This was circulated to his groups for people to work on. It started with something about number. Probably people would have groaned, because they would know that Rodney would be well able to discuss higher maths, so the programme might be rather hard. But no, it wasn't. It started with these very simple words.

> We will study Man:
> As unity
> As duality
> As trinity
> As a play of seven and twelve.

All this sounds quite simple and much easier than all the percentages and fractions and angles I remember having to cope with in school days. And yet it's very profound in it's implications. In fact the whole field of what has become known as "Sacred Geometry" which is the basis of the building of the Great Temple in Jerusalem and of the Egyptian temples at Thebes stems from such basic concepts.

If we take One as meaning a whole, then we can think of "man as unity" when we imagine mankind as distinct from the mineral kingdom, the plants, the lower animals and so on. Each of these kingdoms is a "one" in its own right.

But of course we're not united into one. We fight and squabble amongst ourselves and the world has continual wars. So there are obviously a lot of laws other than the law of one which uphold and maintain mankind.

There are two different kinds of people: man and woman. Masculine and feminine, positive and negative, active and passive rule our lives. So mankind is a duality to start with, divided between male and female.

What motivates us or makes us function or dysfunction in this world? Clearly wars are based on opposing factions, conflicting wills, conflicting convictions. Each side thinks that they are right. In our own individual lives two opposites continually have play. We pull against other people, having different opinions, wanting this or that, being jealous or blaming other people for our own troubles. Disagreement comes from the basic duality in our nature. So from the mass of mankind there emerges male and female and positive and negative. From positive and negative there is always something pushing and something retreating -- or perhaps accepting and then perhaps lashing back in some way.

The Third Force

For a positive and negative to work together in harmony, a third force in necessary. This brings us to the law of three. Rodney said 'as a duality and as a trinity.'

All religions acknowledge some form of Trinity or law of three or triune or triad or triangle etc. The third force is that which unites and makes the two opposing forces work together. As in electricity, where positive and negative need the neutralising force, otherwise they will blow up or just do nothing. We all know this from our experience with electric plugs on our household implements. The third force is that which enables them to unite and work together rather than fight. In mankind, the tension/emotion generated between man and woman can unite them, and the third force may manifest as the outcome: namely, children. The third force is what enables the whole to work, to make something happen.

Christianity has Three in One and One in Three: Father, Son and Holy Spirit. Or of course God the Father, the Spirit impregnating the female, the Madonna. who gives birth to the Son who is himself Spirit in the material form.

India has Brahma, Vishnu and Shiva: the Creator, the

Maintainer and the Destroyer. The Hindu Gunas, or underlying forces of creation, have Sattva the light bringer, Rajas the force of activity, and Tamas the breaker down. The interplay of the three Gunas is said to uphold life.

In the Horoscope chart, we have the Cardinal, Fixed and Mutable signs and the angular, succedent and cadent houses of the chart. None of these threes tally exactly with each other. But they all indicate a law of three. We can also see this in ourselves: body, mind and Spirit; sensory impressions, thought and emotions. And of course the law of three is described when we think of the three wise men. or three wishes, or third time lucky and many other triplicities. People tend to like the number three and feel there's something magical about it.

Also we like the number seven, which definitely feels magical. We can see this in many different places. For instance, the seven known heavenly bodies, that astronomers and astrologers recognised before the time of telescopes. They were the Sun, the Moon, Mercury, Venus, Mars, Jupiter and Saturn. There are also seven base metals: Gold, Silver, Mercury, Copper, Iron, Tin and Lead. By tradition Gold belongs to the Sun, Silver to the Moon, Mercury to the Planet Mercury, Copper to Venus, Iron to Mars, Tin to Jupiter and Lead to Saturn. We have the seven days of the week. In music we have the octave with its seven notes in the tonic sol fah scale: Doh, Re, Me, Fah, Soh, Lah, Te which makes the octave of sound.

Rodney said 'a play of seven and twelve'. So we can look and see where the twelve comes in. Twelve signs of the Zodiac, twelve months of the year, twelve apostles, twelve hours of the day.

It seems we live under some law whereby the One, the Three, the Seven and the Twelve have great significance. But of course there's a lot of significance also to be attached to the other numbers and other groupings of numbers. We have four elements for instance: earth, water, fire and air. Four points of the compass, North, South, East and West. Four seasons,

Spring, Summer, Autumn and Winter.

There's a great difference between the odd and even numbers, and many theories are held about this. Odd numbers appear to me to be the magical and strange ones, perhaps rather feminine, having a lot of possibility. The even ones seem solid, masculine, upholders of the status quo. So we have the Ten Commandments, which give us an indication of how we ought to live. Or the Buddhist Noble Eightfold Path, which shows right thinking, right living, right working, etc. The even numbers seem to be like guidelines to what we should do. We have four corners to the square and we talk about "four square" when we mean straight forward, definite. The strange odd numbers three, five (which by tradition is the number of creativity) seven, nine, eleven and thirteen (which may be either liked or feared) seem to me to be of a different quality. It's quite interesting for instance that the four elements earth, water, fire and air have the rather nebulous fifth element, which I mentioned earlier, according to oriental thought. This can be either space or ether: a concept only.

The Law of Octaves

Gurdjieff said 'All of life is a process, an interplay of different laws. And the musical scale, the octave was invented by the ancients who understood about the basic laws.' Of the law of seven, or the law of octaves, he said that we need to understand that the universe consists of vibrations, in many aspects, many densities, varying directions, crossing and colliding, strengthening and weakening, impeding each other going into retardation, changing direction or even changing their nature.

It is this knowledge that makes all the complications of life, all the implications of higher mathematics, angles, fractions etc. which were so hard for some of us at school. Here also lies the strange law of logarithms, fractional lines of development. Or linkages like the Fibonacchi numbers. These go one, two, three, five, eight, thirteen, twenty one etc.

$$1+1=2$$
$$1+2=3$$
$$2+3=5$$
$$3+5=8 \text{ etc.}$$

The Fibonacchi numbers are found in nature in the growth of leaves on trees, stems of plants etc. Logarithms are seen in, for instance, the fact that a baby doubles in size in a few months and then continues to grow at a lesser and lesser rate until the age of about sixteen. Under the law of logarithms everything slows down, life slows down. A great deal is learned in the first months and years of life and then less and less. Children run about fast, old people move slowly. Life on this earth tends to run down. Think how easily the child learns the basic language that is spoken all around it, but in later life learning a language, even if you visit the country where that language is spoken, takes much longer and is much harder.

Taking the law of octaves or law of seven: the top vibration of any scale, that is the next Doh, is always double the bottom note. But there can't be a simple doubling of the number between one and seven. Because of all the complexities of the vibrations upholding life, the frequency of the vibrations doesn't increase uniformly. Between Me and Fah the increase is retarded, so Gurdjieff said, and again between Te and the Doh of the next octave. This has important implications for us. It's considered theoretically that there are two semi tones between each two notes with the exception of Me/Fah or Te/Doh, which have only one semi-tone. We can't actually hear this because we are so accustomed to the scale, as we know it.

The tonic Sol/Fah scale shows the cosmic law of intervals. A musical scale can demonstrate this but the same law of seven rules our lives much more than we know. And of course three plus four makes seven.

This law is shown in all our activities. The vibrations that start us off on any line of action tend to run down or even change direction. Physics recognises this and the law holds good also in all forms of sciences: light, heat, chemicals, mechanical and other vibrations are all subject to the same laws of development by advancement and retardation. One retardation is always near the beginning and another near the end. Understanding this can explain a great deal about the way we live and the problems we encounter.

Again quoting Gurdjieff: He said, vibrations flow at a certain speed, slow down, tend to break and then pick up again, sometimes in a different direction. This explains why there are no straight lines in nature and no straight lines in our own lives either. And why we are so rarely able to do what we decide to do, and why we don't think in an unbroken straight line. It's the direct effect of retardation of vibrations. We start a course of action on one note, and retardation comes and is a weakening, leading to a change of direction; then a short way forward and another tendency to change. This law shows why, straight lines never occur in our activities; why we start doing one thing and then go on to do something entirely different. But we don't always notice the changes. All this and many of the other difficulties of our lives can be understood by a grasp of the basis of the law of number, together with the understanding and the significance of the role of intervals in each "octave" of our activity. This causes a line of force constantly to change and go to a broken line, turning round and sometimes even becoming its own opposite. We can observe this in what we do.

After a period of strong activity or emotional drive or understanding of what we want to undertake a reaction occurs; the work becomes tedious, fatigue and indifference sets in. We start searching for short cuts or compromises, we avoid or evade problems, we lose interest in the original aim. Sometimes we entirely forget what the original aim was anyway. The line of the octave continues to develop but not in the same direction as before. Work may become mechanical, feeling becomes weaker and descends to the level of common everyday events in life, because the original inspiration has been lost. Our thought may then become dogmatic, literal, no longer having vision, or imagination.

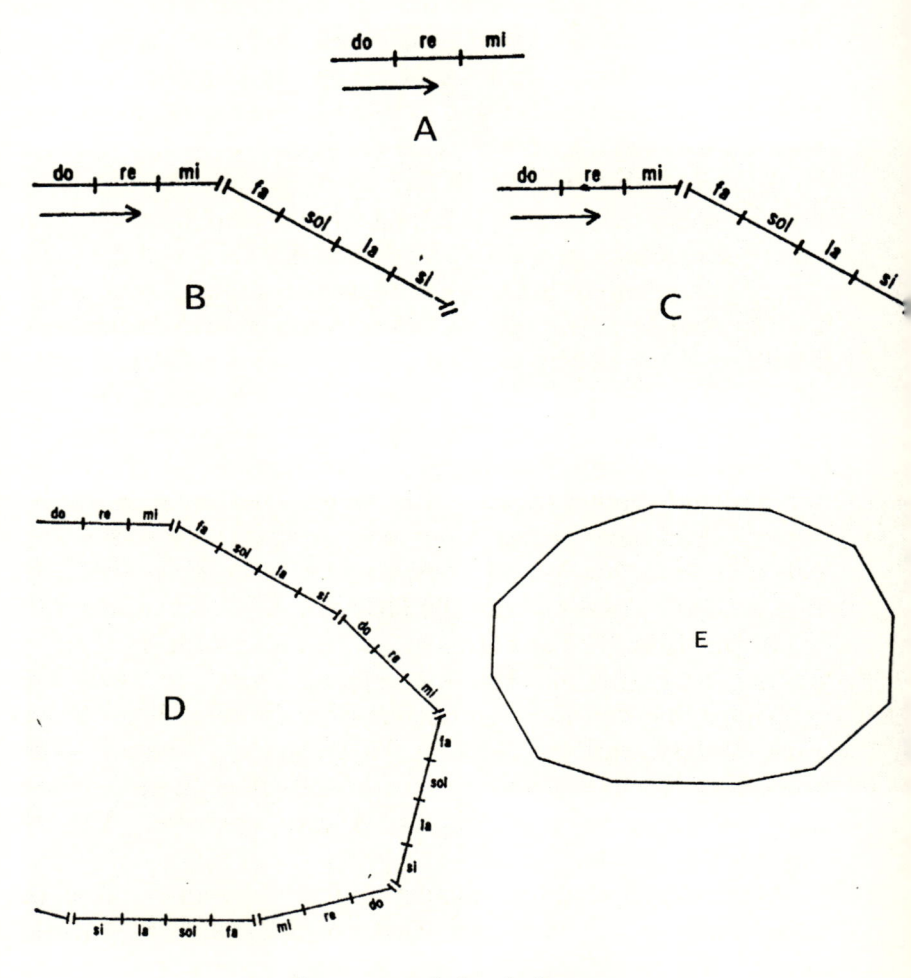

A

B

C

D

E

Octave of Activity

To take a small example. You go out to mow the lawn and then you stop to pull a weed that catches your eye, and then next to the weed you happen to notice a rose that needs pruning. You leave the mower and go to fetch the secateurs from the shed, and then you notice the shed needs tidying and you may start half-heartedly on that. The lawn is not done and after a while you are tired and the sun has gone in and you look at your watch and think it is time to stop. You haven't completed the octave in a straight line. It was turned round on itself. You don't bother with the lawn, you don't even remember that you set out determined to cut it this afternoon. You go in and have some tea instead! Such small examples are magnified in the big ambitious or creative ideas we try to carry out often in vain.

Broken octaves continually cause us to start on one thing and go onto another not realising what is happening. We achieve much less than is possible and often with quite unnecessary outlay of energy and labour.

Achieving our Objectives

Take this book for instance. Perhaps you started to read it with some enthusiasm and interest and read a chapter or two. Then you may have put it down. Next time you picked it up you went on with at least some degree of interest. But before you got to the point where you are reading now, you may have put it down a number of times, or perhaps looked back and forth and onto the last page to see if you can read the secret of life there! You may even leave it for some weeks or some months, and perhaps you will never finish it.

Some people who started reading this book are not even reading these words, because they hadn't got as far before the broken octave took them onto something else. But if you have got to this point, something has brought you back to your original intention. Possibly someone else may have picked it up, started to read it and rekindled your interest in it. Or something occurring elsewhere in your life reminded you of what you found in the early chapters and caused you to pick it up again. So you may indeed complete it, and perhaps it will give you some ideas to take on into life and to make your own in some way. But there must almost certainly have been times when a paragraph seemed a bit long or heavy and you skipped it or were tempted to skip it. It's impossible to write any book where every single sentence is gripping to the reader. There has to be an input from the reader himself or herself; and this is where becoming conscious of the law of octaves and disciplining oneself to go on through the slightly arid times does achieve a very great purpose indeed. We achieve our objective.

It is said that we need some sort of shock to keep us going on through the octave if it is to be completed in the same direction as it was started. Sometimes the shock may come by realising that the book for instance may have been taken out of the library and is overdue back and you pick it up quickly and hasten to finish it. Or something that someone else has said will bring you onto it again. Or you may discipline yourself, simply thinking 'I've set out to read this book and it did interest me and I'm going to complete it.'

It is necessary for people like us to discipline ourselves, to be awake to the need to pass through the "intervals" without much assistance from outside. In real esoteric school work, which is much harder than this, the Master may introduce some shock tactics into what he perceives to be the intervals in anyone's work or activities. The sharp word, the unexpectedly harsh rebuke may be made. Buddhist monks whom we have seen on TV are rapped on the shoulders with a stick when they fall asleep when meditating and they say "thank you". Thank you for reminding me what I was intending to do, for keeping me to my intentions, not letting me wander off, which is so easy when the octave begins to lose impetus. Committed to grow towards cosmic consciousness, the monks submit, by their own will, to a much harder discipline than we would ever be likely to have to accept ourselves.

The same breaking of octaves happens in all spheres of human activity: in literature, science, art, philosophy, business matters, religions, and above all politics. Political parties regularly do U turns as you may have noticed! They come into office intending to do one thing and end by changing their policy with all sorts of excuses and doing something quite different. History shows this fact 'though humanity is far from desiring to notice it' as Ouspensky said when he was commentating on Gurdjieff's teaching on this matter. Wars rarely achieve the ends they were started for, twists and turns happen and the situation becomes different. The same is true of ideologies.

How can Christianity have come from the gospel of love to torturing people in the Inquisition because they did not believe in the love? How many twists and turns of the octave can have led to this? Or to the ideology that Karl Marx developed in *Das Kapital,* changing bit by bit into the brutal tyranny of twentieth century Communism in Russia?

The law of octaves explains many phenomena in our lives which are otherwise incomprehensible. The fact that nothing in the world ever stays the same, everything moves and changes continually; everything is going somewhere, stronger or weaker, up or down, ascending or descending. The inevitable cosmic condition arising out of any action is this continual change, the continual state of flux, a continual swinging of the pendulum, waves rising and falling, energy rising and falling. Our moods become better or worse without any visible reason. There are perhaps a hundred pendulums moving here and there within us: our desires, our intentions, our decisions, are all subject to this law.

This was known to the ancients, who divided time into seven days of the week, with one rest day, to allow for this. The seventh day is the completion of the octave and the beginning of the new octave. In Genesis God made the world in six days and on the seventh day He rested.

In each note of the octave there is also an inner octave and an inner one again in each of the notes. This gives all the depth of our feeling and our emotions and also explains much psychic phenomena.

Will and Awareness

So to complete any task that we set ourselves we have to go back continually to the original vision. We can be aware of our running down and introduce a shock to ourselves if no-one else is there to do it. We can say 'it's running down. I'm getting bored. I'll do something else. Join a Yoga class or learn French or something.' Or we can say 'is the octave complete? What was my intention when I started it? I'll give myself a boost! I'll plough on to the end. I'll get a sense of achievement!' It's just a matter of becoming aware of what is happening.'

The octave can hold its balance through the intervals and the running down if you are aware of it. But how often do we think 'I'll just sit down now and have a cup of tea' and then we don't feel like getting up again so we leave the task for another day! At my age it's very easy to sit down and drop off because I'm very old now and often forget what I intended to do. And of course we must rest and not drive ourselves to exhaustion. But often we wander off thinking 'I'll just do this, or that, as that last thing didn't hold my interest that long' and we are not doing what we intended to do. So we need to discipline ourselves. In real esoteric school we would submit to discipline imposed upon us. To work towards higher consciousness, self-discipline is necessary. It is no good saying 'I promised I would do it, but I don't feel like doing it now so I won't.' Be watchful of "feelings". They can lead you away from your true purpose. So if you find yourself deviating from your true purpose always look back to what that purpose was. A combination of will and awareness is needed for growth of consciousness. Ask yourself what is the first Doh in this octave? And with luck or grace (because help can come) you will complete the octave.

Suggested Exercises

1. Consider the basic numbers and think of examples of unity, duality, the law of three, seven and twelve.

2. Find examples in myths or legends of the traditional meanings of these numbers. For instance three wishes, the seventh child of a seventh child, the twelve labours of Hercules, etc. etc.

3. Look for broken octaves in your own life. Consider the little octaves of every day living and ponder quietly on your long-term aim and ambition in life. Has it changed direction at different times? Do you know where you are going? What you want? Of course some deviations are as a result of life's imposition on us of experience and greater maturity of thought. But it's always a very good idea to go back and ask yourself what was the basic Doh. Then from time to time you will have the pleasure of seeing yourself complete an octave without too many deviations.

TOOLS AND TECHNIQUES

10

Working with the Tarot

It seems to me that there is something that we -- the human race -- can do in this world to further the purposes of the Creator. This seems to involve an attempt to grow in consciousness, so that we fulfil the role so simply described in Genesis, of being both in command of, and in a protective relationship towards the simpler species on this earth, and willing subjects to those discarnate beings who may exist above our own level. I have spoken of this in various ways in the earlier chapters of this book. But I have not until now laid much stress on what I do think is an essential part of this theory: it is, will and intention are needed to a pretty high degree, in at least a percentage of willing and active people, if anything lasting is to be achieved.

Rodney Collin wrote 'it is as unrealistic to think that you will grow in consciousness without effort, as to believe that if you float in a boat down a river you will eventually end up by natural means at the top of a mountain. Obviously this is not the case. If you just float the only way you can go is down, until ultimately you become lost in the vastness of the ocean.'

Perhaps you think this doesn't matter. And if it doesn't matter, then be content to get what appeals to you from this book, or from any other sources. Obviously there are many theories other than mine about the human predicament, and what to do about it! But if you do aspire to reach your higher potential, then it is best to think in terms of Work.

For any kind of skilled work, tools and techniques are needed. Mankind has developed as many tools to enable us to grow spiritually, and achieve some aim, as we have developed tools to work in the world around us, to till the soil and to enable ourselves to live healthily and comfortably on this earth. Most of the traditional 'spiritual tools' seem to indicate the possibilities of a journey from the material or earth level of life, back to the source from which our Spirit came: an ascending ladder or a spiral path to the godhead itself. The ideas may be expressed in many different forms and 'languages.' They may be depicted purely by symbols, which often go beyond the possibilities of words. But basically they are intended for doing something, for getting results from one's efforts.

Most of the 'techniques' involve the use of diagrams or pictures, which can't always be understood easily by the logical mind or by intellectual reasoning.

The best known ones are the Tarot Cards; Astrology, which involves drawing up a Horoscope chart; and the Cabalistic Tree of Life. There are also lesser known diagrams such as the Enneagram, brought to the West by Gurdjieff from an obscure Middle Eastern source, the complex numbers system of the Jewish Gematria and other esoteric type designs or patterns which can be used to enhance and deepen the student's understanding. Their study and use is to enable us to understand what we are and what we may become.

The Teaching Cards

The origin of the Tarot cards is completely unknown. By tradition, the Tarot stems from the mythical god/king of Egypt, known as Thoth, or Truth, as Rudolf Steiner thought the name was more correctly described. There is just about as much reality (or as little historical reality), in the legend of Thoth as there is in the legend of King Arthur and the Knights of the Round Table. They may both have been actual people or the stories may be a bit of an amalgam of recorded memories of various wise men of old, who carried on traditions from 'pre-cataclysmic times' as the Chinese called those days before recorded history began. This is the time before Noah's flood: the period associated with ideas of Atlantis or Lemuria, of Madame Blavatsky's vision. These times, while having no provable basis, occur again and again in one form or another in myths and legends through the ages.

Thoth is by tradition the originator of the arts. He was the inventor of hieroglyphs and simple pictures as a means of conveying ideas, whether inscribed on stone or drawn on papyrus or parchment. They were a way of giving information, to pass on knowledge from one generation to the next.

The Tarot Cards

The twenty two cards of the Major Arcana of the Tarot as we know it today, are thought to have been ancient teaching cards. One may assume little boys sitting at the feet of their father, or students with a Master, learning the archetypal principles that under underlie life, from the pictures and diagrams. They would perhaps learn of love, of loyalty, of duty, of reverence and respect for their fathers and the wise men and the gods. They would be taught that life is hard, that the way forward involves courage and endurance; that there are bound to be clashes of interest; that there would be pain and suffering.. Ideas of right and wrong would be implanted into the young minds.

And the archetypal characters, from the wise old man who is the teacher or father, to the nurturing mother, to the beloved woman who may be partner and give birth to the student's own offspring in due course--all these would be looked at. They would probably look also at such basic archetypes of mankind as the young lover, the eternal rogue, the innocent, and he who has suffered much and lacks the will to continue. The victim figure; the enemy at the gate would also be considered; the process of work, in order to till the land and provide food etc; the nurturing of the young; the need to protect and defend one's self and others, and the paying of tribute to the gods would also be inculcated into the young students' minds.

Ideas of a political or religious kind could also be introduced by this means. By simple basic formulae placed in different orders and different patterns, profound truths could be conveyed about the varieties of human experience.

I think one has to bear in mind that whatever the age or the culture that is using this tool of the Tarot cards, there will always be the archetypal relationship problems of mankind. Even when women are not regarded highly, almost every man knows what it is to fall in love with a woman, and every woman knows what it is to love a man. Likewise, feelings of dislike or hostility are common to everybody at times. Joy, anger, jealousy, grief are all commonplace through the ages, and there will always be a wise man or wise woman somewhere, who bears the torch of knowledge onwards from the fount of experience that springs from the pre-cataclysmic times.

All the 'spiritual tools' can of course give these archetypal pictures of the sort of situations and relationships that man is heir to. But the Tarot alone of the basic techniques I am discussing, has the apparent element of chance in each 'spread' of the cards. The astrological chart changes with the movement of the Heavens, but the basic Horoscope or birth chart does not change. The Tree of Life is contemplated in various ways but the Sephira or Stations of the Tree do not change. They are a framework, for understanding, and any situation or problem can be placed against them. But the Tarot cards are shuffled and it is not known what will appear in a spread. Tarot can therefore easily be debased into cheap-jack fortune telling, and the depths of its possibilities are frequently misunderstood.

Whether the cards are being used as an aid to understanding your nature, or your present situation, or perhaps to help somebody else, it is always customary to use the same procedure. You shuffle the whole pack, and pick a given number of cards after they have been placed face down and fanned or spread out. Anybody who does this will soon discover that some cards tend to come up again and again, while others are never picked. This is a mystery, which is not easily explained, watch and experiment how you may! There is obviously a temptation to believe that something or somebody is manipulating the fall of the cards in some way.

The Lords of the Cards

The old traditions refer to the Lords of the Cards, and there was a custom of invoking or calling upon these mythical Masters, who may help to bring good fortune. Of course, we may think that the way the cards come out is actually pure chance. But those who use them do tend to find that, after viewing and considering a number of spreads, they seem to understand their own problems and their life situation in a strangely deeper way than if they are thinking and pondering in a purely logical fashion. There is something in this 'tool' which is way beyond our normal reasoning powers.

The Tarot as we know it today consists of seventy eight cards. Twenty two are Major Arcana cards, which give the archetypal principles underlying life, and fifty six are the Minor Arcana cards, which fall into four suits. Arcana stems from the word arcane, or hidden. On the whole the Minor Arcana cards indicate the trends and tendencies, the ups and downs of our lives. From these fifty six cards are derived the playing cards which we use today. They were certainly used a very long way back as gaming or playing cards. They are lighter in their implication than the Major Arcana cards.

The first appearance of the two decks together is in fifteenth century Milan. There still exists a complete set of seventy eight rather beautiful cards, hand-painted on embossed leather and apparently originally each attached to a thin wood background. These cards were painted by an artist called Bonifacio Bembo at the request of the Visconti family, who intermarried with the Sforza family. They are known as the Visconti Sforza deck. They were apparently required to play a game known as Tarocchi: hence the name Tarot which we use now.

We don't know what Bembo was actually asked to do, or to design. But what he actually did was to reproduce some ancient picture cards, which already existed in France, and possibly elsewhere in Italy, from about a hundred years earlier. There are still seventeen cards, held in the Biblioteque National in Paris, from a set known as the Charles VI cards. These are much less beautiful, but beyond any doubt, they convey absolutely the same ideas as Bembo's cards.

It seems possible that Bembo may have had some esoteric knowledge himself. Or that the scholarly and well-to-do Visconti and Sfora families, may have inherited knowledge of some sort. They may have been bearers of knowledge from esoteric schools. They may have been playing the game of Tarocchi--but perhaps they were playing the game of life!

The Major Arcana, set out in three lines of seven, will give what appears to be a journey, from a first beginning, through hazards and difficulties to some final outcome. In many ways they show a progression similar to Bunyan's Pilgrim's Progress or the medieval tale called The Journey of Everyman. These are essentially Western stories, and show Pilgrim as an innocent, setting out on a journey to a higher destination. He encounters many trials, hazards, disappointments, and all the pains and ills of life, the cruelties and evils as well as the vanities of human existence. He comes at last within sight of the Celestial City and is reunited ultimately with God from which his Spirit sprang. Earlier cards are sometimes more orientally slanted. There are also American Indian cards which depict elemental deities and influences of pre-Christian or non-Christian traditions, and many other versions of the 'journey'.

There is very much subtlety underlying the meaning of the Tarot cards, and to have a look at a number of different versions of them, especially the older, traditional decks, is the only way to understand the implications of the Major Arcana cards. Of course, they have been copied and recopied many times over the centuries. In the days before printing, they were hand painted, and therefore discrepancies, additions, omissions, variations where a painter has not understood the original intention, have crept in through the years. Many of the decks are rather beautiful; and of course there are also modern versions which can be equally pleasing to the eye.

The Major Arcana

The Major Arcana cards start with **No 0** which is:

The Fool
The Fool is normally placed above the three lines of seven cards each, but can be moved and replaced at the very end, to indicate a return to the First Cause. The Fool is pictured as a young Innocent, having nothing, apparently desiring nothing. In some of the older decks he appears as a Mendicant, in rags. He is quite apparently not part of this world of 'getting and spending,' either at his beginning or at his end, for he is without possessions or attributes of a material kind. When the cards are used for teaching purposes, or with the intention of looking into the future, the Fool stands for carefree heedlessness, with its own hidden dangers. Also, for innocence, impulsiveness and new beginnings. Sometimes he is pictured as a trickster or a jester or a joker: the joker in the playing cards is derived from him. He is an archetypal principal which is 'at home everywhere and nowhere.' Therefore he can be used in the playing cards to trump all the other cards.

After the Fool, we enter the numbered cards.

1. The Magician
This first card appears to indicate the descent of the Spirit into matter. This first manifestation of the Creator is always shown as being masculine in its form. The Magician has in front of him, four tools which are the symbols of the four suits of the Minor Arcana cards. These are the Tools with which he apparently manipulates life on this earth. In a 'reading' -- that is an attempt to use the cards for interpretative purposes -- the Magician stands for the principle of power and the ability to change or manipulate things to one's own advantage.

2 The High Priestess
The High Priestess is the archetypal first feminine principle. The idea of duality comes in at this very early stage; as soon as the unity of the Creator begins to manifest, male and female appear. The High Priestess, stands for pure womanhood, psychic wisdom, intuitive insight into spiritual matters. It is interesting that the male comes before the female at this point, but at the next level, the order is reversed.

3 The Empress
This is the Earth Mother principle, standing for fecundity, abundance, the birth and rebirth process at an earthly level. In a reading she stands for feminine earthly power, abundance, fruitfulness and motherhood.

4 The Emperor
It is curious that at this level the Emperor seems to be subject to the Empress, whereas at a higher level the High Priestess comes after the first masculine manifestation as the Magician. The Emperor stands for masculine power of an earthly kind. In a reading it is interpreted as a benevolent and protective influence, or a powerful man.

5 The Heirophant or Pope or High Priest.
The Heirophant was a Master or teacher with higher knowledge, like the High Priests of old. The Pope, of course, came in to the cards much later and is essentially a Christian invention when the cards were adapted to fit in with Roman Catholic concepts in medieval times. The cards originally reflected pre-Christian and possibly Greco-Egyptian or even oriental thought. The Heirophant stands for help, good counsel and guidance, mercy, goodness and a blessing. This card is the first indication of the need of wisdom and help, and a suggestion that help can come to the Pilgrim who realises his own helplessness

6 The Lover or Lovers

This card shows the tension between male and female. In many old decks it depicted a young man choosing between his mother and his 'mate'. It is taken in a reading as meaning a love affair or strong attraction. Or it may be a major choice or decision.

7 The Chariot

There are many versions of the Chariot, but almost without exception they show the charioteer driving two animals, either horses, sphinxes or mythical beasts, one of which may be black and one white or one red and one blue. The first represents carnal or material desires and the other the purity of the Spirit. One debases, ones exalts. The curious thing is that the charioteer is usually shown as appearing to think he controls the animals. But they are in fact, either lying down or not harnessed to the chariot at all. The charioteer is apparently unaware of how little command he has of the situation. Nevertheless, they are interpreted in a reading as showing the possibility of rapid action.

These first seven cards seem to show innocence trying itself out, the overconfident belief of a young man that he can make things happen his way, before the greater experiences of maturity show life in a different light.

The second line of the cards, which begins to show the difficulties and complexities of life, starts with:

8 Strength.

In the old days this card generally a man guarded by, or in companionship with, a lion, which appeared to be working with him, and the eyes of both man and lion are fixed on the same objective. But later versions of the Tarot have usually brought out Strength in a feminine form--a woman taming or subduing a lion, as though he stood for those attributes in mankind which are subdued by or subject to the feminine in the ultimate. The lion would appear therefore to stand for the base nature of mankind. Later versions became so corrupted that Strength would appear as a man or even as a woman attempting to slay the lion. Strength is interpreted in a reading as the need for courage or endurance.

9 The Hermit.

This indicates the principle of solitude or loneliness. It shows a hooded figure carrying a lamp. It indicates the pilgrim soul realising that in spite of his essential duality, there is a kind of oneness in himself and he can hold steady in his own right. It depicts his ability to stand on his own feet and make his own decisions. But if it appears very frequently, in successive spreads of cards, it may indicate an inability to make relationships. It is the sign of the essential loner in this case.

10 The Wheel of Fortune

This stands for Destiny, in the sense that everything is always in a state of flux: that the only constant is eternal change. It is depicted usually as a turning wheel on which various creatures are always going up or going down. Sometimes they are shown as human beings, but sometimes merely as monkeys at the mercy of Fate. It stands in a reading for destiny, change, and can be problems solved by unexpected developments of some kind.

11 Justice

The Scales of Justice keep things in balance. The picture on this card is similar to Libra, the Scales in Astrology, and shows the need for seeing both sides of a question. It can stand for the Law or for arbitration or litigation. In a reading it indicates things are in the balance, and advises weighing things up carefully. In some Tarot decks, No. 8. Strength (or Force) and No.11 (Justice) are placed the other way round, Justice coming before Strength.

12 The Hanged Man

This is a very strange card, nearly always showing a man hanging upside down by one leg. The other leg is crossed over, this being one of the signs of initiation into esoteric rights. The upside down position is of course one of the Yogic positions, causing the blood to run from the genitals to the head. It is therefore thought to be one of the means of enlightenment in ancient initiation rituals. But in many cultures hanging or crucifixion upside down has been used as the ultimate degradation for a felon. Basically it stands, however, for any reversal in the scheme of things, seeing things the other way round, getting a different vision of life. Conversion, of course, as in the conversion of St. Paul on the road to Damascus, simply means the other way round, the converse. In a reading it is taken as difficulty in seeing the truth. The possibility of misunderstanding a situation. And in the ultimate the need for self-sacrifice in order to gain wisdom.

13 Death

In many of the old cards, Death is shown in a horrifying or gruesome form. Sometimes he is the Grim Reaper, cutting off heads with a scythe, and people are left dying at his feet. In other packs he is a knight in black armour riding a white charger through the assembled multitude. However Death does not appear to indicate physical death or dying. It indicates the end of something, a door closing before another begins to open. The end, or the willing termination of a situation or a relationship perhaps, and the need to look ahead for something different.

14 Temperance

Here is a calm figure pouring water from one vessel to another, suggesting the need for time, a temperate attitude, moderation in all things. The need for control is also suggested. In a reading it indicates hold on, give it time, the problem will solve itself.

Here begins the third and last line, which shows the way out, via maturity and fulfilment. It starts with:

15 The Devil
This is another card which in the old packs was often shown as rather horrifying. Even Bonifacio Bembo's beautiful hand-painted cards show a Devil who is enough to frighten anybody! But in fact he simply represents the strength of the negative. He represents all we mean by the bad as distinct from the good. Sin, as distinct from virtue. The duality manifesting itself in man's actions. In a reading he shows negative influences at play at that particular time, and little progress can be made except by extreme efforts. It can also indicate to the person who is consulting the cards, you are your own worst enemy! You are standing in your own light. You have made these troubles yourself

16 The Tower of Destruction
This seems to stem from the Tower of Babel, which you may remember, fell and crumbled away because it was based on material things--vanities, and not upon the Spirit. It shows a tower falling or people falling from a tower. It is usually interpreted in a reading as a downfall or upheaval, or destruction of plans

17 The Star
Here we see the first unclothed figure of the major cards, kneeling and taking water from a well or pool--perhaps the waters of the well of eternal life. The water is being poured out freely onto the earth. In a reading, it stands for hope and promise and good things for the future. Good prospects. Wishes may come true.

18 The Moon

A curious card which speaks of the waxing and waning, the impermanence of the lunar influence. It often shows a crab, or in its older form a crayfish. This can be identified with Cancer the Crab in Astrology, which in old Horoscopes also looks like a crayfish. And two animals, a dog and a fox or wolf, baying at the Moon. The Moon is often shown as having the Sun behind it or as part of its features, or it may be shown simply in the new moon and full moon phases, one upon the other. In a reading it indicates insecurity or dissatisfaction with the situation. Or fear of the unknown. It is the light of the Moon and not the clear light of the Sun, which shines here, so it is often thought to stand for the occult, the dark hours. It can be interpreted as instability, inconstancy, waxing and waning, continual change. It is a negative as distinct from a positive influence. It can show moodiness, restlessness, unhappiness in the domestic situation. However, it leads on to something better.

19 The Sun

Here is the true light, as distinct from the eerie lunar light, by which no colours can be seen. So Pilgrim, having come from innocence to experience, begins at last to reap the results of his own efforts. The cards generally show the Sun as an unclothed figure, or sometimes as two innocent children, which were originally naked, although at a later stage, little knickers were put on them 'for decency's sake'! This card shows innocence regained and the Sun shines upon them. In a reading it suggests ground for material success and happiness, and all goes well.

Beyond the Sun comes:

20 Judgement

This shows the dead coming alive again, rekindled by the presence of the Spirit. Early Christian cards have the bizarre picture of graves opening and bodies popping up out of them in answer to the last trump! They appear to be ready to face the results of their own past actions. It is as though all can only be resolved finally when this has been done. So in a reading it is tying up odd ends, bringing things to a conclusion, or reaping the results of past efforts. Then comes the final card.

21 The World

This is a partially clothed figure, seemingly an androgyne, neither male nor female. The legs are crossed, the sign of the initiate. And there is about it an air of finality. The journey of Pilgrim is terminated here. It is fulfilment, the end of a cycle of destiny, the point at which the pilgrim moves out of worldly life all together, and is reunited with the attributeless, formlessness of God Eternal, as represented by the Fool. That is, the Creator before He has begun to create the world. The unmanifest. The fount of all things. Innocence regained.

When considering the three line spread of cards, therefore, the Fool can be moved from the beginning to the end as you contemplate it. Here is Alpha and Omega, the Beginning and the End. 'And in my end is My Beginning'.

The Fool has been said to represent God as 'an intelligible sphere, whose centre is everywhere and whose circumference nowhere.'

The Gaming Cards

The fifty six Minor Arcana cards are the ones that became playing cards or gaming cards. They are lighter in tone than the Major cards. They show how the archetypal principles manifest in life. They fall into four suits. These suits are deeply connected with the elements, earth, water, fire and air, as is the case with all the ancient spiritual tools which are intended to help us to understand our own nature.

1 The Pentacles or Coins. These are the equivalent of the Diamonds in the playing cards. They are related to the element Earth, and they stand for material things.

2 The Cups. Equivalent of the Hearts. They stand for the element Water, and they reflect the emotional life, the love life.

3 The Wands or Clubs or Staves or Batons. Equivalent of the Clubs. They are of the element Fire. They stand for the working life, or career or aim in life.

4 The Swords. Equivalent of the Spades. They are of the element Air. They stand for the quality of assertiveness or of aggressiveness.

Each of the four suits of the Minor Arcana consists of fourteen cards: from Ace to ten, and then four picture cards or royal cards. The first of the picture cards is a page or knave, who can be either male or female, and is young. The second is a knight, who is a younger man. The third is the queen, and the fourth is the king. The playing cards have lost the figure of the knight -- which is sometimes however shown as a prince, while the page, or knave becomes a princess. Otherwise they are very similar to the playing cards.

There are many different interpretations of the individual meanings of the Minor cards, but in essence, they indicate the ups and downs of life, and the way all four elements come into play in the course of our activities. The balance of the cards in the four suits is such that almost every possible human experience can be reflected in the way that they fall in a spread. The material, the emotional, the ambitions and desires, the attitudes and so on, are all shown here, reflected against the great Major card archetypal principles which shape our destiny. We are at the mercy of the vagaries of Fate, when the Minor cards come into play. But we can watch what we are doing, and control the events of our lives to some extent at least.

We look to the Pentacles or Coins when we consider money matters, what we can afford, how we are using our financial resources, whether we are by nature frugal or impulse spenders, and how the bills are going to be paid. We look to the Cups when we are concerned with our love lives and our relationships. To the Wands or Clubs when we are thinking about career matters, whether we should change our job, go for promotion, take issue with the boss, or whatever. And to the swords when we are examining our attitude to life or to a given situation. Are we tending to be too aggressive, or too passive; whether we have a right to be assertive in a certain situation, or are we tending to be too much at the mercy of others, for instance.

Each of the 'pip' cards has an individual meaning, related to the element it represents. Different books tend to give different meanings, and for that reason it is much better to stick to one book or to one set of meanings, if you are going to begin to teach yourself how to use the Tarot. In the end you will find that all eventualities are covered providing you don't take a bit from here and a bit from there.

·The Royal or people cards tend to show the principles manifesting through the various people around us: our family and friends, work colleagues and those we have dealings with.
Because the interpretations in different books vary so much, people often feel it is almost impossible to master the Minor cards at all, and they tend to want to work with Major cards only. This is a complete misunderstanding of the significance of Tarot. It depends essentially on mastering and understanding all the cards, and using major and minor ones together.

The meanings of the Major Arcana cards is pretty well indisputable. Of course they are very ancient, and not therefore anything like so debatable as the meanings of the playing of gaming cards--which tend to be interpreted in terms of the customs and culture of the times in which they are being used.

The use of the Tarot is essentially to understand ourselves, examine our motives and purposes, and learn how to make the best use of 'the hand of cards' that Fate has dealt us this time round. It is often debased into a mere fortune telling device, in an attempt to find out what will happen, who one is going to marry, or what you or somebody else will do, or what will take place next. But this would imply that they convey a cut-and-dried fate in which we would have no possibility at all but to react like automatons to a given situation. There seems to be little reality there.

Rightly used, they give great insight into one's own nature, and into the natures and characteristics of the friends and people that one deals with, and the situations that we find ourselves in. It is a misuse of this ancient and most valuable tool to play with it, using it as a trivial game, or trying to look into the future by means of it. It is a much better usage of the cards to get hold of one or two different decks, study the pictures, and read at least one book about them.

The older decks are much more difficult to understand and interpret, because the pip cards of the Minor Arcana, consist entirely of geometrical designs and not pictures at all. Many occultists hold that this is very important. The believe the effects of the mathematical patterns that are formed in this way, are of enormous significance and have and have an actual effect on the brain when they are contemplated or meditated on. However, for practical purposes I generally advise getting the Rider Waite cards, which were published first in 1906. These are much used and have pleasant Edwardian pictures for every card. They are the ones that are commonly seen on television in plays where the Tarot cards are shown. However, some of the older cards may appeal to the seeker after truth.

There are about 250 different decks of Tarot cards available nowadays, some of them being bowdlerized versions of older decks. Some are modern ones drawn by people who have in some cases superimposed their own ideas upon the ancient tradition. It does sometimes seem that something has been lost, in many of these contemporary decks.

You will need to learn different ways with spreading the cards, if you are to experiment with them at all. There are many very good books on this subject. I would always recommend that good scholar Rachel Pollack, who has written a number of books about the Tarot, but there are also plenty of others.

Rightly used, the tool and the technique of the Tarot cards can be a very great help to understanding

Suggested Exercises

1. Enquire around and see where you can buy Tarot cards in your own neighbourhood. They are much more readily available now than they were a few years ago. Get the Rider Waite deck, and one or two more decks that attract you, if you feel you can afford them! They are not cheap. Perhaps about £15 a deck.

2. Get one sound-looking book and read it. Experiment with it and see whether this seems to be a tool that you yourself can use with pleasure and advantage.

11

The Qualities of Time

Astrology is a study of the qualities inherent in any given moment of time. Of course, mostly we acknowledge that time has no reality in itself: it is just the way that we perceive things in this world. As the philosopher Flammerion said, 'yesterday, today and tomorrow are man-made concepts. In the heavens it is always today.' All the same, we all know what we mean by the days of the week and the months of the year, and the hours shown by the clock. This is our way of recording our experience of the turning of the planet earth on its own axis, and what appears to be the rising and setting of the sun, giving day and night, due to this rotation. As the earth tilts a little on its axis we also get the changes of the seasons. We know when to expect winter, and when the days will get longer and warmer in Spring, as our part of the earth is tilted a little more towards the sun during the summer months.

The philosopher C.G.Jung wrote: 'We are each of us born in a given moment of time, and like vintage years of wine, we bear the qualities of that moment in which we were born. Astrology lays claim to nothing more.' This is a very good way of putting it. So often people imagine that astrology is simply a fortune-telling device, and that if you can find out what is in your horoscope chart, you will know what is going to happen. In fact this is not so. A horoscope chart, set up for a known actual birth time, date and place, is extraordinarily accurate in explaining what sort of person it would be, that as a newborn baby gave the first cries of protest as it was brought into the world. Whether it would be, for instance, a gentle and unassuming person: artistic and creative: dominant and ambitious: whether with certain talents or the tendency to just let the world go by.

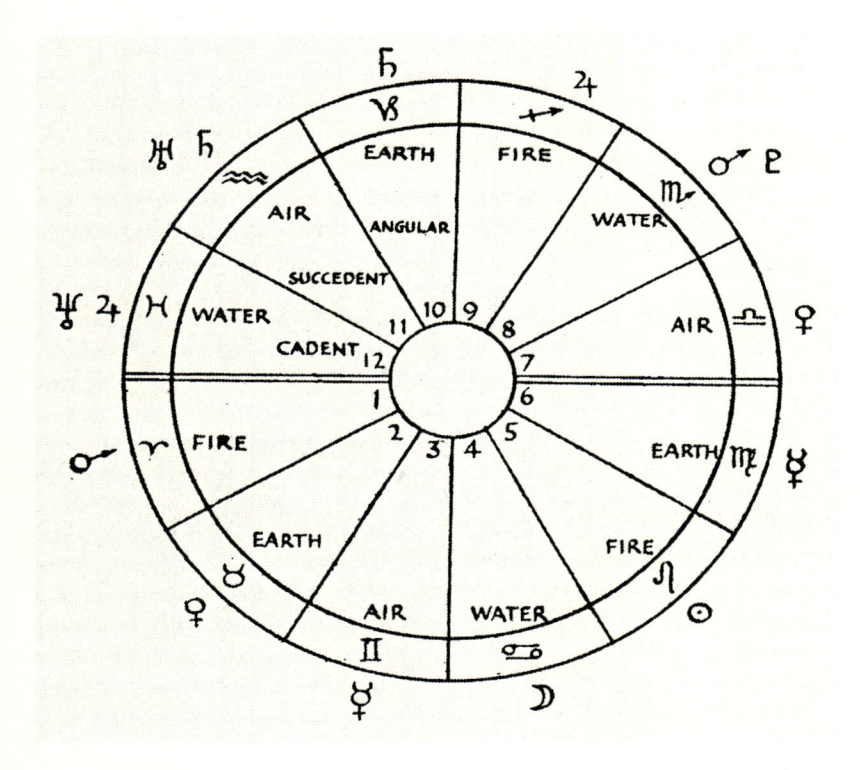

The Elements in Astrology

It appears that the qualities of the given moment of time in some way correspond with the qualities of the creature that takes its first breath in that moment. It will be true to some extent of any creature--a puppy being born at the same time in the kitchen for instance! But as much more can be expected of a child than a dog, one will see this manifesting in a more limited way. A quick-tempered impatient child, a quick-tempered impatient dog: a nice cuddly ingratiating animal, a tactile and biddable child!

Some people have been known to 'order' their pets from a litter that is going to be born at the right time of year to be compatible with their own birth charts. I know an astrologer whose Siamese kitten had to have a little horoscope set up before being accepted as the right one to buy from the breeder. She found Leo a beloved companion who seemed to understand everything she said or did. When his life came to an end,. she set up a chart for a newborn litter to make certain of another good choice. She named him Bigcat, and he turned out to be so like Leo that she felt he might be a reincarnation of his predecessor. She had looked for and found the same qualities and characteristics, that blended happily with her own.

It is not always understood that astrology concerns our own solar system: that is, our sun and the earth and all the other attendant planets that circulate round our sun, which is itself moving along its own spiral path within our galaxy, the Milky Way. The great constellations, which we can see when we look up into the heavens on a clear night, are much, much further away from us than the planets. But we use twelve of the constellations as guidelines or marker points, to give what we call the Zodiac.

The ancients used the Signs of the Zodiac for travelling or navigational purposes. Being so very far away from us, they always appear to hold their own positions relative to one another, and to rise and fall at certain times of the year. So they could always be relied upon to be where the experienced navigator expected them to be.

But from very early times, there seems to have been a tradition that the Signs were also associated with certain types of person. We don't know where this knowledge came from. It would be true to say that, just like the Tarot cards, and the other 'tools and techniques' as I am calling them, this knowledge goes back to pre-cataclysmic times. That is, before Noah's flood, into a time when secret knowledge was apparently available on this earth. Though much was clearly lost, bits and pieces of it remain here and there in these old traditions. By looking at them and trying to make use of them, we may be helping to rebuild the tumbled ruins of an ancient edifice and make it whole and habitable again. That is one way of looking at it.

The Twelvefold Zodiac

Here in the West we have always used a twelvefold Zodiac. I'm sure you are quite familiar with the names of the Signs--Aries the Ram, Taurus the Bull, Gemini the Twins, Cancer the Crab and so on. These are constellations among many constellations that are visible in the heavens. But they are particularly the ones that are traditionally picked out as making 'guidelines' that divide the heavens more or less evenly into twelve sections. Other ages and civilizations have had other Zodiacs -- that is, they have chosen other constellations. They have always included some of the same Signs, though the names vary a little. In India, for instance, there was a twentyfold Zodiac. Mexico also had twenty Signs. Some of the ancient Oriental Zodiacs have been much greater. Korea, for instance, had a Zodiac of forty eight Signs.

This doesn't means of course that anything has been invented or changed, or has deviated from what is actually visible in the heavens. It simply means that certain constellations have been pinpointed and recognised. It is nonsense to speak, as the media did recently, of a new 'Sign' having been discovered, when Ophiocus was pinpointed and discussed. It has always been there, always known, but not used by Western astrologers, that is all.

One of the very interesting things about the different Zodiacs is that the names bear so many similarities, although they spring from so many different ages and cultures. For instance, in India the Sign which we call Aquarius the Water bearer is Kumbha the Waterpot. And our Capricorn, the goat with a fish's tail, is Makara the Crocodile. It is impossible to know why so many of the same Signs have been repeatedly picked out and given the same or similar names: and with the same qualities attached to them.

Some authorities suggest that this is simply a case of cross-culture spreading of ideas, and that maybe the whole thing was simply invented by mankind and the knowledge passed around. But this does not appear to bear investigation. The distances both in time and place seem too great, and I am one of those who ascribe to the belief that higher minds than our own are behind the complex and beautiful art of astrology, one of the sciences of the ancients. A common source would seem to be the most likely explanation. But what that source may be is quite beyond our memory or our understanding.

When we talk about the sun or the planets being 'in' a certain Sign, of course we simply mean that as our earth turns on its own axis, we see the sun rise against a certain Sign of the Zodiac for one month of the year. The sun is said to be 'in Aries' between about April 21 to May 20. In Gemini from about May 20 to June 21. And so on. Because the constellations are so far out in space and planets are much closer to us, going with us round our sun. It seems to us as though a planet is in a certain Sign, when it is simply in fact passing through the heavens with that Sign in the background. The Signs seem to us to be static, out there so far distant through space and time -- and the space/time concept it in itself very difficult to understand -- whereas the planets, and particularly the moon, seem to us to move continually relative to where we are ourselves.

The moon appears to move through all the Signs of the Zodiac within one month. Mercury and Venus take about one year to go through all the Signs; Mars two years; Jupiter about eleven and a half years; Saturn nearly thirty years; Uranus takes about 84 years -- perhaps roughly one man's life span. The outermost planets, Neptune and Pluto are slow-moving, because they are further away, and may remain for many years in one Sign. They therefore never repeat their positions within anyone's lifetime.

The Planets as Gods

In Western Astronomy and Astrology, the planets are known by the names of the Greek gods.

The small planet nearest to the sun is named after the messenger of the gods -- **Mercury**. He flew about the heavens bearing messages and conveying knowledge from the gods to each other or from the gods to man. Where he is in your horoscope chart will therefore indicate something to do with communication or travel or movement. Mercury strongly placed in the birth chart is likely to indicate a lively, possibly garrulous personality; somebody who has a facility with words or who likes to be on the move.

Venus is the next planet outwards from the sun. Venus was the planet of love and harmony. The placing of Venus in your horoscope chart will indicate your love life. She likes warm relationships, and a happy lifestyle will be cultivated. Venus also shows quite an interest in creature comforts and in money.

Next comes **Mars**, the god of war. Where Mars is placed in the birth chart will show the degree of forcefulness, energy, drive or even aggressiveness in your nature.

Further out in space is the enormous planet **Jupiter**, the god of plenty, of acquisition and success. Strongly placed he may show ambition to succeed. Jupiter is a mature and positive figure, enabling you to take things calmly and with reasonable optimism.

Saturn is the old, cold god. 'The characteristics of Saturn in the birth chart are those of limitation, restriction, a tendency to seriousness or even depression.. He leads to wisdom and calm in old age.

These were the only planets known to the ancients, but of course we have the three extra-Saturnian or outer planets known to us and now used in Horoscope chart. They were only discovered after telescopes came into use, and Pluto in fact was only detected for the first time in the early twentieth century. They are not discernible to the naked eye.

Uranus is thought to be associated with disruption, upheaval, revolution, rapid change. In Greek legend he slew his own father.

Neptune, named after the god of the oceans, is to do with nebulous and non-material matters; the emotional or the spiritual life.

And further out in space, **Pluto**, the god of the underworld, is associated with endings and new beginnings. He is sometimes thought of as being the god associated with death, but generally the influence shows itself this way only in the sense that when one door closes another opens on a different set of circumstances. A strong Pluto may bring a life of endings and new beginnings.

The ancients also thought of the sun and the moon as being planets, though of course we know now that the sun is our master in a manner of speaking, for our earth circles round it, tied to it. And the moon is our own attendant or satellite, for it goes round the earth.

The **Sun** is associated with Apollo, a shining and positive influence in the heavens. Therefore a positive influence in the horoscope chart. A strongly placed and unafflicted sun will lead to a strong, optimistic and positive nature.

And the **Moon**, having no light of her own, takes the light of the sun and is the feminine to the masculine, according to ancient tradition. She is the negative to the positive of Apollo the sun god. She waxes and wanes, a fluctuating and changeable influence in the Horoscope. A strongly placed moon in your chart will accentuate the feminine characteristics, whether in a man or in a woman, whereas a strongly placed sun will accentuates the masculine or positive -- the duality again. The Moon can be said to represent the shadow side of ourselves, whereas the sun may represent the reality, which perhaps we can't always easily take.

By ancient tradition the planets represent the life principles, which move and activate us. We all experience the pull of Venus every time we fall in love or every time the emotional side of our nature is stirred. The need to communicate, to talk, to move, comes from Mercury. All forms of anger--the wish to defy someone, for instance--can be said to spring from the Martian influence with Mercury also involved. Getting and spending comes through Jupiter, and the caution of old age shows when Saturn has full play. Any doubts and depression are Saturnian, of course, at any age!

These principles are in a continual state of flux, for the orbits of the planets round our sun vary in speed, and in the distance they are from the sun and from each other. So they make a rather beautiful, ever-changing pattern, which never repeats exactly, because it has so many different permutations.

The Twelve Human Types

The influence of the planets is played out against the Signs of the Zodiac, which by our Western tradition, have twelve different characteristics. These are the characteristics which are associated very strongly with the number twelve: twelve different types.

Aries the Ram can be a bit of a battering ram! The Arien type is on the whole forceful, perhaps even a but pushy, tending to ride roughshod over other people, always wanting to get somewhere, to have their own way.

Taurus the Bull is a rather home-loving, possessive type, tending to value possessions and to like the comforts of this life: food and drink and all good material things are pleasing to the strongly Taurean person.

Gemini the Twins has characteristics of changeability, lively, having very little staying power. Geminians sparkle on social occasions, and with new friends or acquaintances is one of the dual Signs of the Zodiac..

Cancer the Crab is a maternal Sign, protective and caring, but tending to hold on to and control others. While being feminine and maternal in many ways, strongly Cancerian people are often quite devious. The crab walks sideways!

Leo the Lion is the king of the forest--a proud and upright figure, liking to be in the limelight. Leonians naturally assume the lead in most circumstances and take it for granted that their voice should be heard. There is a warmth and openheartedness about a Leonian character.

Virgo the Virgin is neat, precise, can be a bit inclined to be pernickety, nit-picking over trivialities. Virgoans are often much concerned with the minutiae of life, whereas Leonians see the broad picture. It is quite interesting that Virgoans often have a neat, small handwriting, while the Leonian hand tends to be large and bold.

Libra the Scales is another Sign with two qualities--the up and down, the weighing property of a pair of scales. It is associated with justice and the law, which is itself represented by a figure of Justice bearing scales. Librans tend to see both sides of a question, to weigh up one thing against another. They are on the whole bridgebuilders or peacemakers between opposing factions. Librans usually enjoy the arts and have a strong feeling for colour, shape and so on. But there is a lack of the neatness and precision which characterizes Virgo.

Scorpio the Scorpion has a sting in the tail. Scorpionic characteristics are those of playing their cards close to their chest. They don't open up easily. There is often an intense depth of feeling. They can be a bit suppressed emotionally, uptight, and have difficulty in leading a relaxed type of life. The sting in the tail can be a sharp and caustic tongue.

Sagittarius the Archer is shown as a man to the waist and the rest of the body is that of a centaur, half man half beast. Sagittarians are open and outgoing, like social contact and travel and can be interested in sports and athletics.

Capricorn the Goat, with the tail of a fish, reaches from the mountain tops where the mountain goats spring from peak to peak, to the depth of the ocean. Capricorns have endurance and courage, and tend to keep going no matter what the difficulties of a situation. They like to achieve their aim, but they do tend to swoop from great elation to black despair-- very much at the mercy of moods.

Aquarius the Water Bearer has unusual likings and interests, and often something unusual about the appearance or mode of dress. Aquarians sometimes have a desire to be seen and to present themselves in a showy way. They pull against the accepted order of things, and may make a rather good contribution to life because of their individuality and originality.

Pisces the Fishes is a dual sign, gentle and unassuming on the whole and tending to want to look after or serve others rather than to want to be seen or heard. They have little wish to lay down the law or make a big contribution. The weakness of Pisces is their difficulty in facing issues or standing firm in difficult circumstances. Like the slippery fish, they slither away and are not to be found when anything tiresome is going on.

We take the Signs of the Zodiac from Aries to Pisces, because it is the Sign Aries against which the Sun rises at the Spring equinox. We have to start the Zodiac somewhere, and we start it therefore at that point, when the days are lengthening, with the summer ahead -- rather than at the beginning of the calendar year.

You will recognize the twelve Signs as describing more or less twelve different types of people: such as the twelve apostles, all different types of mankind. And various other twelves we have mentioned.

The Horoscope Wheel

The Horoscope chart looks like a wheel with twelve spokes. The chart is divided into twelve Houses, the first house being always half way up on the left-hand side. To see what a Horoscope actually represents, you will need to think of standing out of doors looking towards the sky. If you look to the south, the sun will rise on your left-hand side and go down on your right, passing more or less overhead, but lower and lower in the southern sky as the winter sets in, and our part of the earth tilts a little away from the full glory and strength of the sun. We thus have a chart with the East on the left and the West on the right, the south at the top, north at the bottom: contrary to normal maps and diagrams.

The **Houses** of the chart represent the fields of human activity.

The **first House** represents your personality. The **second**, the money and close possessions. The **third,** the intimate family. The **fourth**, the wider spread family, the bloodline so to speak. The **fifth** is the House of Creativity, love, and the sex life. If there are a lot of planets in the Fifth House, there will be a lively, creative personality, possibly with a vigorous sex life! The **sixth** is the House of health, the physical body, the limbs. And also by tradition any servants of, or people subservient to you. So a full sixth house may indicate somebody who gets into a position of power and employs others. It may indicate a tendency to health troubles. The **seventh** House is the House of marriage or partnership. The **eighth** is the House of death, or, in a strange way, money or possessions which come to you from sources such as legacies--not money which is earned. Earnings are generally shown in the second House. The ninth is the house of travel and movement out in the world. The **tenth** is the career or work in life. The **eleventh** is the house of social activity and friendships. And the **twelfth** is the inner side of your nature, your emotional or spiritual life at a deep level, even your subconscious motivations. By tradition it can also be the House of self-undoing. If you look at the diagram, you will see that this is taking you round the chart in an anti-clockwise direction.

The Turning Circles

The chart needs to be seen as an ever-moving, ever-changing organism, not just a flat diagram on paper, to make it have any reality for us. We need to think of the Signs of the Zodiac moving in a clockwise direction, coming up over the horizon on the left-hand side, going up into the heavens so that at about midday the Sign that was on the left at sunrise, will be near the mid-heaven. It will be down over the western horizon at sunset, and at the bottom of the chart at midnight. This of course is simply a means to show on paper the way things look to us. It is actually our own earth turning on its own axis, which gives this impression of the Signs of the Zodiac actually rising. It is the earth itself, which is turning continually. The clock simply reflects the apparent movement of the heavens.

Now the planets appear to be moving predominantly anti-clockwise through the Signs of the Zodiac--except when they are traveling in retrograde motion. Of course, none of the planets actually turn and suddenly go backwards through the heavens. But retrograde motion is what we seem to see when a planet appears to be going back relative to another planet or in the Sign against which it is observed. This is rather like traveling along in a slow train when a faster train goes rushing past. We get the feeling that our own train is going backwards. It's just the way things look to us, and is caused by the varying speed of movements of the planets. Except when a planet is in retrograde motion it is moving continually, but at different speeds, from one degree to thirty degrees of each Sign. Any circle, of course, is divided into 360 degrees as we learned in our maths classes at school. So there are thirty degrees in each Sign. So the planets are moving anti-clockwise and the Signs rising clockwise. The Houses are always static, the first House being always on the left-hand side. So you can look through the spokes of the wheel, as it were, with the two turning circles beyond it, one clockwise and one anti-clockwise.

The interpretation of the Horoscope chart depends not only on understanding the meanings of each Sign and of each planet and each House--three different lists to learn! It also necessitates being able to interpret the meaning of any planet within a given Sign within a given House. And also, relative to the other planets in the chart. The angular relationship of one planet to another is extremely important.

Planets which are within eight degrees of each other are said to be **in conjunction**, and will strengthen each other. Planets which are **in opposition** to each other in the chart, will tend to impede each other. A ninety degree or **square** aspect can be a difficult one, whereas 120 degrees, which is called a **trine** aspect is on the whole a benevolent one, as is a sixty degree or **sextile** aspect. These are the main 'aspects' but there are many more fine gradations, giving the minor aspects, which also have to be looked at in considering a Horoscope chart.

So the principles of Mars, (action) conjunct Venus (love) for instance, could mean going full tilt into a love affair. Mars in opposition to Venus might cause a bit of a love/hate relationship. Mars square to Venus may indicate impediments and difficulties in trying to get a relationship going. We also have to consider which Signs of the Zodiac these planet are 'in' and where all the other planets are at the time, in order to analyse any given situation.

The Subtlety Within

You will soon see that to learn to use Astrology properly means a very great deal more than simply looking at Horoscopes in your daily newspaper! Newspaper so-called Horoscopes of course, have practically no reality at all, although they should, as a general rule at least say which Sign the Sun is in on a certain date and give some generalized indications of the overall trends on that date. But they can't be relied on to give you anything real about yourself. A real study of Astrology takes a long time: in fact one can study it for years and still find more and more subtlety and beauty within it.

Subtlety and beauty is found in the real use of all the 'spiritual tools' if you are sensitive enough to experience it.

This is also the case with a few very ancient games such as chess, which in some way seem to represent and emulate the 'game of life.' A friend of mine who played in and won chess tournaments confessed that he had great difficulty in choking back tears as a skilled opponent played him and he would suddenly 'see the beauty' of the next move he would make.

The mind is capable of much greater subtleties of thought than we realize in our day to day activities.

If you can learn to set up a Horoscope chart, even in a very simple and basic form, you will see how the characteristics of your friends or of yourself can be seen very clearly. However you can't tell easily what will actually happen, except by deducing it from the natal trends and setting this against what is known as a progressed chart. That is, a chart which shows where the planets are, and in which Signs they are, at this time.

A skilled astrologer will be able to tell which times are propitious for action; or whether trying to do anything at that time may result in you 'banging your head against a stone wall.' Some periods of time can be seen in advance to be not very favourable and therefore to be looked at with caution, wide awake and attentive to the possibilities. Others have a very marked 'go ahead' look about them: times of advancement in your life or of good things to be achieved. But even in a good year, consciousness and will seem to be needed to get the best out of the gifts that fate seems to offer. Rashness or big-headedness may mean that one makes a bit of a hash of things all the same, and only realises later what the realities of the situation were.

The astrological world, is full of stories of disasters experienced by people who thought they could avoid the planetary influences in some way. And who are generally seen as being thwarted because they failed to realize that the influences would be there anyway, and it is a case of how you actually face up to them.

There is a traditional tale of an astrologer in medieval times who, seeing that his chart looked very unfavourable, resolved to go to bed and have nothing to do with anything, then he couldn't come to any harm. However, while lying in bed he heard somebody out in the street crying 'Fire!' In a panic, he leapt out of bed and rushed out of his bedroom to see what was going on. He fell over a pail which a housemaid had left standing on the landing and fell from top to bottom down the stairs and broke his leg, so the story says. So he would have been safer in his ground floor living room after all!

There's a more modern one, which a friend of mine vowed was true though I could not verify it. A business man was warned by his astrologer that he could lose his very considerable wealth, under prevailing aspects unless he was very cautious in his business dealings. He decided to go away entirely and leave his two sons in charge of his business, knowing that they themselves were not under the same unfavourable astrological aspects and could be relied upon. He went down to the south of France and lay in the sun. Then getting bored one day, he wandered into the casino and idly watched the play. In the course of the next week he gambled away his entire fortune.

These may well be apocryphal stories. However I don't want to suggest that we are bound to suffer the full bad effects of difficult aspects in our Horoscope. On the contrary, astrological tradition says 'the fool is ruled by his stars. The wise man uses them.'

'Sweet are the Uses of Adversity'

The use of the possibilities of the planetary aspects and the understanding of the uses, even of difficult trends, may be part of the art of growing in maturity and understanding. 'Sweet are the uses of adversity', as Shakespeare said. If the aspects are not good you are unlikely to win the lottery. But then you are unlikely to win the lottery anyway. It is simply a case of avoiding, during a no-go period, the temptation to put more than you can afford into that bottomless pit in the hope of changing your fortune to your advantage. At such a time you probably won't even win a tenner!

Looking for a good period to start a new project can be very worth while, however. Astrological bodies, or others who understand these things, do sometimes choose a suitable date and even time, to form a new business or company, or start some new lines of action. This means that they will ask an astrologer to set up an **electional chart** and meet on that date. An **inceptional chart** on the other hand is the chart of the date and time on which things are deemed to have been started. Occasionally a big project which seems to have been started with high hopes but which runs down badly, may be seen to have been started under very unfavorable aspects. It would be interesting to see an inceptional chart of the Millennium Dome project! It would have to have been set up to show the date, time and place when the first moving spirits of the idea began to formulate them and put them into written form for government perusal. Such a document would be hard to come by.

Bodies like the **Astrological Association**, and the **Faculty of Astrological Studies** and the much older **Astrological Lodge of the Theosophical Society**, were all set up to electional charts prepared in advance, to show the most favorable time to get them off to a good start. On the whole these bodies have kept going and flourishing very well, and have shown their forebears to have been well-advised in their choice of date.

Astrology used to be recognized in medieval times as being a suitable subject for university studies, and it was of course known much further back as an important discipline, used by the masters and teachers of the young. Astrological artifacts found in the valleys of the Euphrates and the Tigris, buried now largely under the desert sand of Iraq---an area fought over during the Gulf War--go back about 4,000 years. It is amazing to find Signs of the Zodiac carved on boundary stones, for example: the same Signs that we use today. Egypt also has very many ancient artifacts, which are quite clearly astrological.

It is impossible to know how much of this strange, ancient science and art is actually manmade. Just as it is impossible to know how much of the tradition behind the Tarot cards, or of the Cabala and the Tree of Life, comes from mankind's own gropings, to understand his own nature and find means of helping himself.

There is often a tacit assumption that higher minds than our own must originally have invented the technique of setting up and interpreting a Horoscope chart such as we know it today. To understand that people learned to navigate by the stars and the planets is quite easily acceptable. Whether traveling by camel across a wide desert or in a small unstable boat at sea, it would always be possible to look up at the heavens and recognize the same great clusters of stars and use them as signposts to the East or the South. But how did we ever know that a person born at sunrise with the sun in Aries and Mars on the Mid-heaven, for instance, would tend to be an outgoing, even rather aggressive person? And that his nature might lead him to become a soldier, traditionally wielding the sword? Or a doctor using the surgeon's knife? These things were known by Ptolemy, the Greek philosopher, whose writings on astrological as well as philosophical subjects are quite extraordinary and valid even today.

The Great Ages

When we look at the long term picture, we find that the astrological Great Age of roughly 2000--2.500 years, has also a profound significance. This is the time which is taken by the poles of the earth's axis to complete an entire circle round the pole of the ecliptic. This is due to our oscillatory movement, rather like the swinging motion of a spinning top. We are just coming out of the **Piscean Age** and entering the **Age of Aquarius**. The actual entry into the new Sign takes a long time, over a hundred years, so the people who make much of the idea that we are in the **Age of Aquarius** now, are rather jumping the gun! The Aquarian Age will not reach its full flowering for a good many years yet, but its influence is beginning to be felt.

The **Piscean Age**, the age of the fishes, has been characterised by Christianity. Christ was portrayed as Icthus the fish--a symbol found carved on stone in the catacombs in Rome where the persecuted early Christians took refuge and also in some old churches and monasteries. And Christ was born of a virgin: Pisces the Fishes and Virgo the Virgin lie opposite one another in the Horoscope chart. Virgo the Virgin is also associated with the Greek goddess of grain, the Earth goddess Demeter. The parable of the loaves and fishes has often been recalled in this connection.

The previous **Great Age** was that of **Aries the Ram**, (about 2000BC), The ram, seemed to dominate thought and the legend of Abraham and Isaac and the ram in the thicket stems from this time. The Greek goddess Pallas Athene was armored and wore ram's horns on her helmet, and Roman soldiers had the same. Christ was later known as the Lamb of God, the offspring of the ram.

In the **Taurean Age** (about 4000BC), the Bull was held sacred, and the legend of the Israelites and the worship of the golden calf seems to spring from this period. Sacred bulls are shown on carvings, both in Egypt and in Mexico dating from this far off time. The Greek legend of the Great Bull of Minos fits in here.

The **Geminian Age** (6000BC), had a prevailing cult of twins. Sacred pillars dedicated to pairs of gods were found in Assyrian and Babylonian temples. Rome had Castor and Pollux, and Romulus and Remus the twin children were by legend the founders of the ancient Eternal City known as Rome.

The **Cancerian Age**(8,000BC) saw the beginning of the Moon Goddess cults.

The **Leonian Age** (10,000BC) has left some mark in the very ancient lions' faces found in South America in the remains of temples thought to have been dedicated to worship of the Sun. The Sign Leo is ruled by the Sun, and it seems possible that ancient ideas and legends of a sunny, golden age for mankind come from as far back as this. Perhaps this was the pre-cataclysmic time of Chinese tradition.

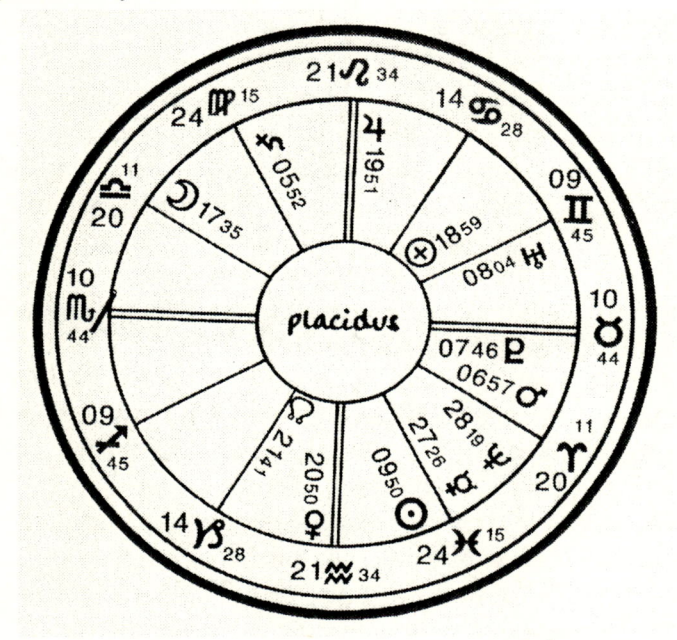

Rudolf Steiner, February 27th 1861
Kralijevic, Austria, 10.06pm (GMT) approx

This was the chart Steiner used as his own. But it may have been his baptismal chart. An intense introverted natal chart, showing strong spiritual leanings, a desire for knowledge, a strong will and a wish to serve others.

    The Ages appear to go back instead of forward through the Zodiac, because as astronomy shows, the slow tilting of the earth over the ages causes what is known as the **precession of the Equinoxes**.
    The Aquarian Age, as we begin to enter it, shows a marked tendency to throw away an attitude of servitude or submission--Christian characteristics of the obedient sheep being led by the Good Shepherd in the Piscean Age. And to

move on to a determined 'I am my own master' attitude among people in general. Fine, if we all take responsibility for our own development and pull our weight in the world of our own volition. Not so good if it is a defiance of any sort of authority and a 'me first' attitude which cares about no-one's interest but my own! It is curious and interesting that the growing demand for self-determination pushes through against an increasingly authoritarian and 'bossy' attitude by governments everywhere. Aquarius the Water Bearer, may well auger the greater availability of the water of the Spirit, enough for all, not just for the chosen few. It is ruled by disruptive Uranus however, promoting change, revolution, upheaval--all the violence and overturning of old customs and accepted principles which we see as we move into the new century. But Uranus is also concerned with waves and rays, electricity, speed of communication; and many of the scientific advances, such as the increasing rapidity of travel. The advent of computers, e-mail for communication etc., tally of course with these attributes. It has been pointed out that the first rooftop TV aerials were identical in shape to the glyph used for Uranus--certainly a curious coincidence!

There is so very much in the use of the science--incomplete and inexact though it may be -- and the art of interpretation, that belongs to the astrological tradition, that study and understanding are needed if you want to make anything much of it. Sun Sign or star Sign Astrology is nothing at all by comparison with the real thing. But from this rather short résumé you may feel that this is another of the great spiritual tools that can aid our understanding of ourselves and our possibilities and of the nature of life.

Suggested Exercises

1. It is worth while paying a qualified astrologer to set up and analyse your Horoscope chart. You will need to know an approximate birth time, though the astrologer will discuss

with you ways of getting round the problem to some extent if you don't know the time at all. Without a birth time, the astrologer can't be sure of your Ascendant or Rising Sign, on which your personality depends, or the angles of the chart. But the planets, other than the fast-moving Moon, can be calculated well enough. **The Faculty of Astrological Studies at FAS BM 7470 London WC1N 3XX**, is the principal teaching body, although there are a number of other reputable schools or correspondence courses. The Faculty would send you a list of qualified consultants, all of whom have the diploma of the Faculty and can be relied upon. There are also several other teaching bodies and individual self-taught astrologers who would undertake this work. However it is not cheap. Expect to pay between £50-£100 for a detailed written or taped analysis. You may get an hour's consultation and a brief analysis for much less.

2. When you know what is your Sun Sign and Ascendant and you have got at least a simple, basic chart which has been analysed for you, see how you can relate this to your own nature as you understand it to be.

3. There will be Astrology classes somewhere in your neighbourhood. Many local authorities now run courses, and it is worth while to consider joining one.

4. There are enormous numbers of astrological books to enable you to study further for yourself. Your local bookshop or public library can help. There is a great wealth of ancient classical works, and many good modern works. It is impossible to recommend more than a few, but I would draw your attention to **The Principles of Astrology**, by Charles and Suzi Harvey (Thorsons,) a good paperback by the late Patron and former longterm President of the Astrological Association: and **What Astrology can do for You**, by Stephanie J.Clement, (Llewellyn/Airlift) an excellent little book for beginners.

12

The Tree of Life

The ancient diagram known as the Tree of Life is generally associated with the Hebraic teaching known as the Cabala. But like the other ancient tools and techniques, it comes from so far back in time, that the origins are completely unknown The word Cabala simply means that which is 'received,' or given by God. There are three basically received religions or religions of revelation. They are Judaism, Christianity and the teachings of Islam. It is interesting that they all claim Jerusalem as their own: their Holy City, their revered place. It seems probable to me that this area of the earth -- Gaia, Mother Earth -- may be one of the strongest, or perhaps the strongest of the power spots; so greatly loved, desired and struggled for that it is for ever being fought over by its troubled and troublesome children! In this place where the Dome of the Rock, the Great Temple, and various temples and shrines seem almost to spring spontaneously from the rocky hillsides, very many esoteric teachings and holy writ of all the religions seem to have originated.

The Tree of Life is central to Cabala, but appears in other forms, not only in the West and Middle East, but in the Orient too. It is a deceptively simple picture of a tree with a central trunk and branches. It is said to represent Mankind, or God, or the entire Creation, with the Creator existing in unmanifest form outside the diagram itself. Man is the microcosm to the macrocosm: that is the small to the large cosmos. We have the same properties, being made 'in the image' of God.

Some of the early versions show a rounded or whole Tree

with various creatures or properties depicted on or at the ends of its branches where the fruit or flowers of a real tree would appear. But the more familiar Cabalistic version is a flat diagram with a central column, two outer columns, circles depicting the 'stations' of the Tree and paths linking the stations one to another.

By tradition this Hebrew version stems from Abraham. He had grown up in the Old Testament period of belief in one almighty, ferocious God, who punished His children if they didn't do as they were told. Then he had some sort of revelation, which caused him to want to look beyond this simplistic view of the Creator. He went to see Melchizedek, the King of Jerusalem. It seems possible that Melchizedek was a 'Schoolman,' in the sense in which I have used this word before: a man who had knowledge stemming from an Esoteric School of some kind, which carried on secret ideas from the Pre-Cataclysmic times.

The Ark of the Covenant

Abraham is said to have learned from Melchizedek, and whatever he may have learned, he turned into the core of his own future teaching to the people of Israel. He made a pact with God that he would keep faith with what he had learned. He seems to have taken on board a vast complex of ideas suggesting that God is in everything and everywhere, and that Man's journey back to the source requires understanding and will. Whatever Abraham then wrote down, or carved on stone, or in some way committed to a tangible form, then became the 'Covenant' with God. The Ark of the Covenant, which contained whatever Abraham had placed in it, became a Holy possession, carried before the Children of Israel, wherever they travelled in their wanderings in those early days. Its exact numerical measurements and description were recorded, ascribed to God's instructions to Abraham, and it was believed therefore to be a source of power, to be venerated and feared.

What happened to the Ark in later years has been the subject of much debate. It has been claimed to have been found on various occasions. The most recent one was when Hitler believed he had located and acquired it. He believed this would give him complete power over the Jews, and ultimately over the world.

A recent book, 'The Sign and the Seal' by a diligent researcher, Graham Hancock, suggests that it came to rest long ago in Ethiopia, at a place called Axum, and that it exists there still, guarded secretly by priests. Ethiopia was for long a Christian country, of course, until Communism swept old traditions away, but it has a pre-Christian Hebraic tradition. There are Ethiopian Jews, dark-skinned, known as Falasha Jews, who claim their descent from Menelek, son of Solomon. Many strange, mystical traditions still hang on, in that now chaotic land.

The Children of Israel, guided by their priests, knew of Holy Writ but the ordinary people were unlikely to have been privy to what exactly Abraham's Ark of the Covenant actually contained. They were still taught of the wrath of God and lived in fear of Him. The secrets of the Cabala were revealed to very few, 'elite' people. But no-one however highborn or scholarly, was allowed even to study The Tree until he had lived long enough to be of mature understanding. It was said to be too strong a meat for the children!

It is true of course, that knowledge, as distinct from mere information, can be dangerous in the hands of the immature or the power-seeker, which is why it is not generally for sale in the market place. It is almost the truth that people need to acquire information for themselves, and begin to turn it into knowledge for themselves. Only then may they, by luck or by grace, receive a taste of real knowledge as a revelation or a gift.

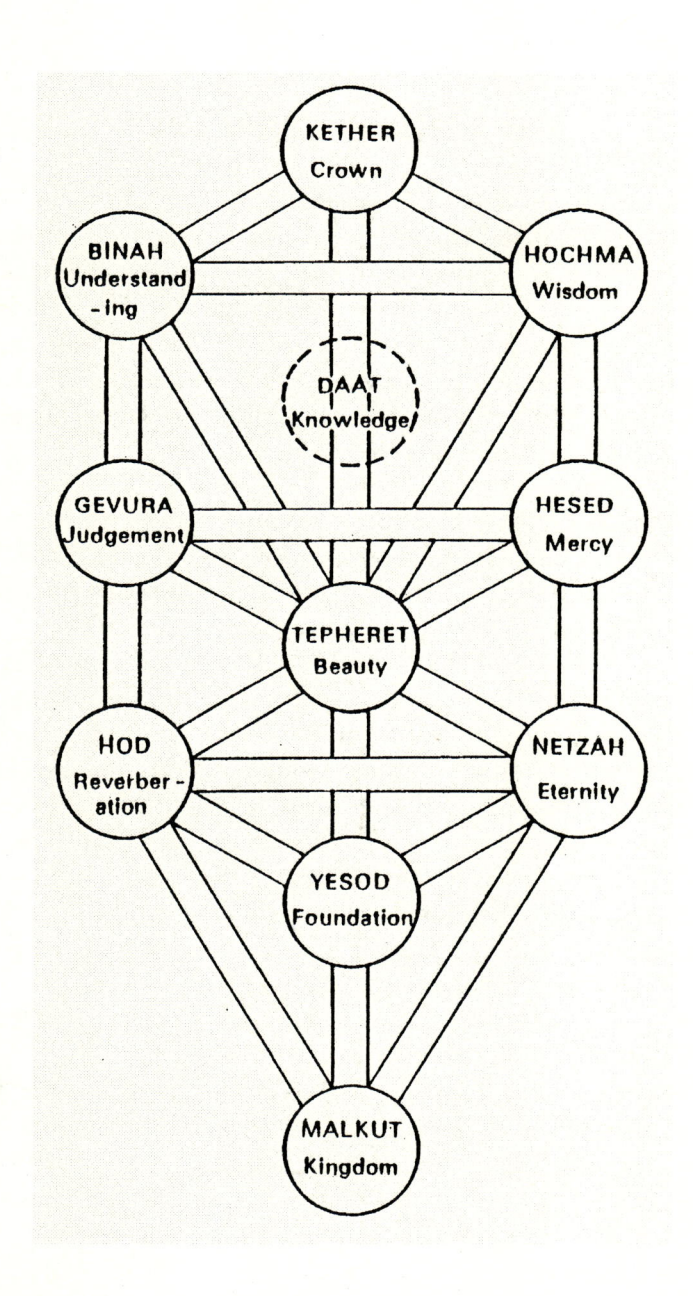

The Tree of Life

The Stations of the Tree

The secrets of the Tree reveal themselves little by little. First we look at the diagram and see the central column or trunk which is known as the column of balance or equilibrium. At the very top is Kether the Crown. This is the first of the **Sephiroth** or Stations of the Tree. There are ten Sephiroth, and another nebulous Sephira, (the singular of Sephiroth) which exists only in the initiate or more advanced student, or in certain times or conditions.

At the base of the Tree is Malkut the Kingdom. God manifests at Kether, and the emanations from the godhead breaks at once into the duality of positive/negative, masculine/feminine, which we have seen throughout all the disciplines.

On the right-hand side is the positive or Column of Force. On the left, the feminine or Column of Form. The emanation or power is thus in a continuing state of flux, swinging between two extremes of manifestation, steady only when on the central column. All life is said to manifest in this way. And an understanding of this essential basis of Creation, makes it easier to see why we find it so difficult to hold steady in our own lives. We change our opinions, encounter different circumstances encouraging us to change our viewpoint, are drawn into varying relationships with others, and in many everyday ways, deal with the positive and negative, masculine and feminine within our own natures.

Only when we can function from a central point on the Tree, are we able to see ourselves and our situation from a balanced viewpoint. But inevitably, soon the swing is going to begin again.

The names of the Sephiroth are ancient Hebrew, and very difficult to translate, which is why different versions of them are found in the many scholarly books on the subject. I take the versions given by Z'ev ben Shimon Halevi, a Sephardic Jew who has also written under his English name of Warren

Kenton. His deep understanding of Cabala stems from initial teaching by his Grandfather, and the considerable number of books he has written in the last thirty years have made Cabala acceptable and understandable to a wide readership.

The translations are: **Kether** (the Crown). Down one step on the right, **Hochma** (wisdom.) Paired on the left, **Binah** (understanding.) The next pair are **Hesed** (mercy) and **Gevura** (judgement.) Centrally between these two pairs is **Daat** (knowledge) which is the Sephira which, on the centre column, is not linked by any pathways and exists only at a higher level of development.

The next pair are, on the right **Netzah** (eternity) and on the left **Hod** (reverberation.) Above and between these two pairs is **Tepheret** beauty). Tepheret is on the centre column and is linked to all the Sephiroth except Malkut. It is a centre point on which, occasionally, we may hold ourselves steady and see the objective truth about the situation. It is a point of great power, which we can aspire to function from, and certainly aim towards as we attempt to understand the Tree.

Below Netzah and Hod, and also central is **Yesod** (the Foundation) and below this again, **Malkut** (the Kingdom).

Kether is the first manifestation of the Absolute. Above this level is the Unmanifest, Attributeless, impossible for us to define at all. By Hebraic tradition, beyond Kether is Ain Soph Aur, Limitless Light. Beyond Ain Soph Aur is Ain Soph, Endessness. And beyond even Ain Soph is Ain, the Void. The ancient definitions stretch the mind, enable the vision to seek what can't be grasped by the intellect -- the concept of endlessness, of absolute nothingness.

At Kether the Crown is the Spirit manifesting in its purity and wholeness. Encountering the first law, it opens at once into the duality that we are familiar with: positive/negative, masculine/feminine. And from this point down, the interplay of the two forces, their interdependence, their lower and higher forms, and their increasing complexities, lead via the descending branches of the trunk of the Tree, to Malkut the Kingdom. This is, broadly speaking, the point at which we recognise ourselves: our bodies made of, and living through, the elements: the minerals of our bones and sinews and fleshly form, the water which circulate in us in the form of blood and fluids, the fire which is drawn from the heat of the Sun and keeps the heart beating, and the inhaling and exhaling of the air, without which we can't sustain life at all.

And yet the Spirit seems to manifest there at Malkut as well as at Kether and throughout the Tree, enabling us to have that gut feeling that the essential 'I' that we recognise inwardly, is surely more than this earthly body. The Spirit manifests through the Tree of Life, so we must have at least a spark of it in ourselves.

The ideas developed through the Tree are a great deal more subtle and interesting than the simple journey of Bunyan's Pilgrim, struggling manfully onward from the City of Destruction to the Celestial City, via hazards and setbacks that require rugged endurance and little more. The traveller on the Tree learns that all the attributes of the author of Creation are available to help him, if the will and the hunger are there in sufficient degree. And he finds that help may well be available, as his understanding grows.

The Lightning Flash

By tradition the first force or emanation from Kether descends via the Lightning Flash, crossing and re-crossing the Tree, from Sephira to Sephira: Kether, Hochma, Binah, Hesed, Gevura, Tepheret, Netzah, Hod, Yesod, Malkut. It does not, however, take in Daat, which seems not to exist, to be a potential only, and to be much to do with growth of consciousness. It is said that, of all created forms, Man alone has the possibility of going straight up the Tree via the central column, encountering Daat on the way. But mostly we tend to swing, to wobble, to veer from side to side, experiencing the positive and the negative in all that we do in life. We are a mass of contradictions in our actions and out ideas, and find it exceedingly hard to keep on an even course. Therein lie all the argumentativeness and cross purposes and indecisions and changes of mind: all the quarrels, battles and wars that mankind seems to be heir to. And yet there does seem to be a possibility of growing beyond our continually troubled state, and holding more steadily to our vision or ultimate goal.

The Tree of Life is such a profound subject that one can well study it for years, reading many books and meditating on the significance of each of the Sephiroth and of the paths that link them. I give you only this simple outline, as a very significant spiritual tool that has been inherited from way back in time.

All the twenty two paths linking up the stations or Sephiroth are living, moving possibilities, while the Sephiroth themselves are principles which just 'are', which exist unchanging throughout. One may put the Archangels on the Sephiroth, if one wishes. Or the planets. Or the Tarot cards. Or the octave, starting with Doh at Kether and descending to the final Doh at Malkut. None of these other ways or disciplines will tally exactly, but the same principles can be seen throughout. With the Tarot, it is the Minor Arcana cards which sit on the Sephiroth, in groupings by number, (all the Aces at Kether, etc.,) and the Major cards on the paths, for it is the underlying principles of the Major cards that give us our possibilities.

If we concentrate on Tepheret, Beauty, we see that it is linked to all the other Sephiroth except to Malkut, from which it is separated by Yesod. Tepheret can be thought of as our Sun, or as Apollo, or as St. Michael, Lord of Hosts. If we could function from this point, we should have many easier possibilities of growth. But mostly we tend to work from

Malkut, shadowed by Yesod which represents the Moon, and acknowledging the shadow more than the Sun itself. Of course, we can look directly at the Moon with our naked eyes, but not at the Sun, which would blind us if we did so. This in itself may be of significance. The practical use of the Tree lies in being able to place one's self, in one's meditations, on Tepheret, seeing possible courses of action from that centre point, when considering our lives and our work circumstances, our relationships etc. See which way the paths lead. Am I leaning too much to the right or to the left, (not politically of course).

To initiating (or Forcing) a course of action, or to an obstinate determination not to budge, (Form) for instance. It may be quite interesting to consider whether the Right and Left in politics somehow corresponds. in essence, to these profound ideas in our experience.

The Four Worlds

The Tree is also shown as incorporating four worlds, which overlap each other. From Kether spring Aziluth, the world of Emanations. This overlaps with Briah, the world of Creation. This in turn overlaps with Yetzirah, the world of Formation. And at the lowest level Assiah, the world of the Elements and Action.

The idea of four interlinking and overlapping worlds occurs in other teachings, including that of Rodney Collin. His four worlds were called the Electronic Realm, the Molecular Realm, the Cellular Realm and the Mineral Realm. They were thought to develop by a logarithmic time scale, from the very slow speed of the mineral level to faster and faster speeds. He spoke of them also as Heaven (Electronic), Paradise (Molecular), Earth (Cellular), and Hell (Mineral). All the realms are described as co-existing, and can all be experienced within ourselves as we reflect the great laws that hold throughout creation.

The Tree is seen as so enormous, that it may also be depicted in an extended form, the Kether of one Tree being only the Malkut of the one above. And in the lower regions, Malkut may be Kether of yet another realm. There can therefore be seen a Tree with a concept so vast that there is neither beginning nor end to it.

We can all see a little beyond Malkut. If anyone moves a little from Malkut, presenting him/herself as having some purpose, all the glories of Tepheret and the possibilities of the Tree begin to open up for the would-be traveller on the Way. But many people are quite content to spend their whole lives in the basic triad of the Tree, moving around from Malkut to Yesod to Hod, or from Malkut to Yesod to Netzah and back again, which enables all the getting and spending, the arguing and repetition and making and breaking of friendships and relationships to go through a lifetime, without anything further ever being glimpsed or even desired. Remember the little girl who burst into tears at the fruitless activity of counting beads or sorting building blocks? She already glimpsed something further -- a better and more long term aim.

If there is some desire to achieve something, to create or to understand, then possibilities open up as soon as a person is sufficiently motivated. For example: supposing you want to write a book. You have an idea or a vision of what you want to do -- and visions in their essence come from Kether, the open crown through which the Spirit flows. But the practical carrying out of the intention has to start at Malkut, with all the nitty-gritty work of getting your equipment, your pen and paper or word processor or whatever, and the laborious business of getting on with it. Yesod sees you, yourself, looking to assemble and sort ideas at Hod, to go on to Netzah and look deeper into your purpose. Tepheret brings a vision-of-the-vision so to speak: a renewal and wider understanding of the ultimate purpose. Gevura looks into and judges what has been done so far. Hesed has a renewed force of energy as the book is coming on. Binah and Hochma give the final assessment and the book is finally brought into being at Kether.

Experimenting with the Tree

I experimented when, following the death of my husband, I decided to sell the house. To calm my inner turmoil of grief and thoughts about the future, I was trying continually to meditate my way up from Malkut, station by station, to Tepheret on the column of equilibrium, and to hold steady there. Continually I watched myself slipping back to Hod, thoughts going round and round in circles, always culminating in 'Why doesn't the house sell?' 'Why can't I get on?' This was linked, of course, to the Foundation and the Kingdom, the land where the house actually stood. From time to time I slipped across to Netzah, which had seen it all before, which knew that this was all part of a bigger cycle of events in my life. I had moved house before. I might possibly have to move house again It takes time to go through all the ramifications of moving house, and I needed to wait calmly for the time to be right.

I then saw that I was on a bigger triangle, with both columns of the Tree recognised in the process. As the thing progressed, I needed to be linked to Gevura, which caused me to ask myself whether I had made the right decision to sell now? To weigh up possibilities and make judgments without agitation. If I could look round about from Tepheret, the long-term purposes and inner significance for me would seem quite clear. And looking beyond, I felt assured the understanding and wisdom would be there in due course, and would see me through to the finality of my move to a new place for my next years.

By repeating the exercise during those difficult months, I found I could deal with estate agents, viewers, my lawyer, my own search for a new home, and the actual move, by bringing my attention back continually to the actual moment, and the qualities of the Sephira or Sephiroth from which I was functioning. The principles of buying and selling would always be at Netzah. The repetition of the routine of showing the house to potential purchasers was at Hod. Dealing with the contract, at Gevura. And as I searched for and recognised my new home, I tasted Hesed. As I asked: 'How am I to manage, all on my own?' I centred myself again at Tepheret and saw that fresh energy and impulse would carry me through. When considering the whole structure of the Tree, I saw my own past, present and future life reflected there.

Inevitably old age lay ahead, and with my attention on Binah (understanding), and Hochma (wisdom), I have attempted to work towards the Highest. Maybe through the looking glass of Daat, I have from time to time had a brief glimpse of my essential Self.

'The Tree is an Analogue of the universe and man,' says Halevi. 'And we are at the meeting point between heaven and earth. We are an unrealised Tree in miniature, and we have the right to travel back whence we came.'

Suggested Exercises

1. Review what you have read in the Tools and Techniques section, comparing one 'spiritual tool' with another. When might you use the Tarot cards? What would you hope to find in the Horoscope chart? Under what circumstances might it be appropriate to consider the Tree of Life?

2. What have all these techniques in common? Are there times when it might be a good idea to use more than one of them?

3. As with the other major tools, reading further on the subject is the only way to begin to work seriously with the ideas behind the Tree of Life. I suggest any of the books of Z'ev ben Shimon Halevi, because he has taken ancient ideas and written about them in a way that is relevant to life today. But there are a vast number of other books on Cabala which can be found in any library or good bookshop. Have a good browse!

13

The Way of the Carpenter

There was an old carpenter in the village in Oxfordshire, where I spent some of the years of my early childhood. I remember being taken into the dusty interior of the workshop, when I was quite little. I was told to wait there, near the door while my father did some business with him.

I stood looking around. All along the walls, high and low there were tools of all kinds, some of them hanging individually on hooks, some in rows on shelves, or in groupings or in pullout drawers. They ranged from the enormous two-man saws which were used in those days to cut up great tree trunks, before the time of chainsaws, down to the tiny little fret saws for carving intricate pieces of furniture, delicate scrolls or fancy bits. There were hammers, from the huge lump hammers for fencing posts or heavy hardwood, to teeny-weeny hammers for use in tiny corners and for very small fine nails. There were chisels, screwdrivers from the coarse to the fine, bradawls for making holes, tools for fastening one thing to another, dozens and dozens of them. They were all shining and clean and neatly placed in order, so that the carpenter could turn at any time and put his hand on the appropriate tool for the job that he was doing. Of course, I didn't know at that time, what they were all for. But it seemed like a strange and interesting magical place.

Later when I was bigger, we children would sometimes stand in the doorway and just watch what was going on in the carpenter's workshop. I came to realize that evidence of his work could be seen everywhere in the village, from cottage floors and steep staircases, to shelves and cupboards and drawers. In the bigger houses carved mantels, lintels and banisters might have been made by him or by his father before him, and the old manor house showed evidence of the work of his forebears.

We were never allowed to put a foot beyond the threshold of the inner doorway, and a sharp voice would command us to go away if we ventured further. But Aldwick, as he was called, was not a hard man, for he had a kind twinkle in his eye. I would watch him bent over the bench, my gaze going from the old head with its shock of gray hair to the bare brawny arms with, I remember, a dragon tattoo on one of them, to the skilled old hands moving lovingly over a piece of wood as he smoothed or sanded or polished, working and turning it this way and that, intent on his task, using the many tools with the skill and experience of a lifetime of practice. It would have been nice to go nearer, but we were in awe of him and stood still. No doubt, he knew very well how mischievous little fingers would touch and play with everything. And of course, apart from the inconvenience to himself, there would have been danger in the tools, so sharply honed and professionally kept, if they got into young hands.

Fresh from Sunday School teaching, it occurred to me one day that Joseph was a carpenter, and the child Jesus must often have watched a scene like this. But only in recent years, did I realize that there might be deliberate symbolism in this story, just as there is profound symbolism throughout the Gospel tales. The fact that Joseph had a craft that equipped him for life, to earn his living and to take a place in the world, and that Jesus himself would be expected to learn that craft, seemed to me to have great significance.

I have often thought that possibly what we have to do in this world is to become skilled craftsmen of some sort, learning to use the tools of our trade, whatever particular craft or trade we may decide on. In a manner of speaking, there are suitable tools for everything we may do -- though not necessarily material ones. They range from the big, heavy 'tools' like shouting, or anger, that we use when strength or force seems to be needed -- or perhaps when we find ourselves bludgeoning our way along, for better or worse, when life gets difficult! To the fine, fiddly little tools that we need, to handle with tact or finesse, gentleness or kindness, some problem or relationship difficulty. Perhaps what we have to do is to learn the 'craft' of living, and acquire the appropriate tools to fashion what we desire or what we need. We could grow in skill through the years, moving from clumsy apprenticeship to confident maturity, and later perhaps into a mastership of some kind.

Working with our peers in the Workshop of life, we exchange the satisfaction of companionship, the ability to see and consider and perhaps admire another's work. And every now and then, perhaps in a moment or despondency or doubt, or even in a flash of happiness, we may seem to feel the living breath of a master craftsman at our shoulder, or imagine the touch of an experienced hand guiding our own less assured one in some way.

Tools of our Trade

If we are working our way through this world, then the tools we need first and foremost are the tools of the material world: all the many, many material tools that we use every day, from the knife and fork with which we eat our food, to the car or train which gets us to work, to all the complexities of the word processor and the computer at the office. At home we feel we need our vacuum cleaner, our cooker, all the inventions that are usual today. Though our forebears managed with simpler tools of living, until the need to expedite matters in some way led to ideas and developments that could make every day living easier.

Apart from material objects, in the few million years since man first walked upright and learnt to use a stone pick to dig, or a club to enforce his will, intellectual tools have also developed Our primitive ancestors may have used only simple and gruff communications. There might have been a rapid resort to violence, leading to the survival of the fittest, and may the devil take the hindmost. This gave way, at least in theory, to discussion and negotiation and exchange of ideas for mutual benefit.

The Tools of the Magician:
Pentacles (Earth), Cup (Water), Wand (Fire), Sword (Air)

Of course, even nowadays we often neglect to use our finer tools -- skilled and patient negotiations -- and resort to the heavier and simpler ones of shouting and screaming to achieve our ends. Hence the quarrels and the wars. But we do know that there are better tools on the workbench, with which to fashion something of mutual good. We have the ability to use the tools of patience and forbearance, and attention to the other apprentice craftsmen who sometimes need another pair of hands.

We can perhaps consider the great range of our tools, and try to use the best that are appropriate. For this, time and experience are needed. For instance, irony and wit are sharp and useful little tools in sophisticated hands. But sarcasm has a cutting edge that can rarely be usefully employed.

As we are working our way through this world, of course we need to learn to use, with skill, the social tools of the world, as well as the many trade and business and practical skills that enable us to earn a living.

But if we are also treading a spiritual path, we would do well to learn also to handle some of the spiritual tools that our forebears, the ancients from far off times of which we know so little, bequeathed to us.

As already described, Tarot, Astrology and the Tree of Life are probably the best known of the major spiritual tools that we have inherited. But of course, there are many others.

The **I Ching** or Book of Changes, is an extraordinarily profound, although seemingly very simple book of ancient Chinese origin. It is used for a method of divination involving the use of yarrow sticks, or coins. The drawing of long or short sticks, or throwing of the coins will give a number referring the user to any one of sixty four hexagrams in the book. Each of the hexagrams describes a situation, then the kind of people involved, and then the probable outcome. To 'throw the coins' to help one to understand and deal with a problem can be extraordinarily revealing!

The first version of the I Ching dates from very early Chinese history, and no-one knows the origin of it. There have been later adaptations down the centuries, and it is still used very much today. Although the people and situations described refer to a simpler culture than our own, they are so archetypal in their essence that they are perfectly comprehensible, and can easily be applied to our own problems.

Cheirology, or the study of the hands, also originated in ancient China. Hand reading, or palmistry as we know it in the West, is not really quite so old or anything like so subtle. Western palmistry has been carried via the Romany tradition, itself stemming originally from India, and of course a common source is just possible. The nature and character of the person can be interpreted basically, by studying the hand shaping--which is linked to the four elements. A broad palm and short fingers gives and Earth type. A long palm and long fingers is a Water type. A long palm and short fingers mean a Fire type. A broad palm and long fingers show an Air type. The skin texture, the way that the fingers lean, the dermatoglyphics or lines and markings, and many other factors are examined and analysed, in considering the nature and characteristics of different people. As much can be seen in the hand as in the Horoscope chart.

The hands change much more than we generally realize. If you examine your palm over the weeks, months and years, you will see, how even the basic lines alter with the years. The past, present and even trends and tendencies for the future, can be detected by the skilled practitioner.

Casting the **Runes** is a delightful practice, which stems from ancient Norse tradition. The meanings of the twenty two runes, which are generally carved on little blocks of stone or wood, deal with the basic life principles or types, and archetypal situations. The throwing or casting of them will give a pattern depicting the events or situation of the present time, and the probable outcome, as well as giving some indication of what needs to be looked for to improve things. There is no indisputably authoritative book on the meaning of the Runes. But Ralph Blum's *The Book of Runes* is probably the most commonly consulted today.

Numerology. In it's present day usage Numerology strikes me as having the tantalizing incompleteness of the tumbled ruins that so many of the occult arts have become. It is based on a linkage of numbers and letters of the alphabet. Each letter is assigned a number between 1 and 9, and these single numerals each have a specific archypel significance.

This tallies with a statement in *Foundations of Tibetan Buddhism* by the Lama Anagarika Govinda, that "originally every letter represented an idea". The Cabala has the same tradition with regards to the Hebrew alphabet, the 22 letters of which have each a place on the Paths of the Tree of Life.

While Numerology may have had deeper meaning once it tends to be regarded as a simple form of fortune telling or looking into the trends and tendencies of a person or situation.

Commonly, the letters and words are set out in two lines. There are several versions, the most used being attributed to Pythagoras BC55.

A B C D E F G H 1 J K L M N O P Q R S T U V W X Y Z
1 2 3 4 5 6 7 8 9 1 2 3 4 5 6 7 8 9 1 2 3 4 5 6 7 8

Only the figures 1 to 9 are needed, so add together all letters of the name or word and reduce them to a single figure as below:

P E T E R J O N E S
7 5 2 5 9 1 6 5 5 1

46 = 10 = 1

The numbers 1 to 9 represent characteristics similar to astrology, thus:-
1. Aries, Scorpio. Mars.
2. Cancer. Moon.
3. Taurus, Libra. Venus.
4. Aquarius. Uranus.
5. Gemini, Virgo. Mercury.
6. Sagittarius. Jupiter.
7. Pisces. Neptune.
8. Capricorn. Saturn.
9. Leo. The Sun.

You are therefore finding the archetypal principal inherent in any name or situation you ask about.

There are other and more complex ways of setting out the numbers, stemming from esoteric and particularly Cabalistic tradition. Personally I have never found today's versions reliable. I tend to feel that there is an underlying reality in Numerology but so much has been lost that we cannot entirely trust the versions we have inherited.

Feng Shui (pronounced Fung Shoy). This is definitely an occult art and is enjoying great popularity at the present time. It involves aligning one's house, furniture and possessions in such a way that good and helpful vibrations are picked up from the compass points. And ultimately from the angular relationships of N, S, E and W. It does therefore seem to be related to this Earth rather than to the Heavens. Benign influences, are believed to be attracted by using the traditionally correct parts of the house for specific purposes. And there are hints for keeping malign influences at bay.

Many people have had their house "Fung Shuied" by experts and feel they have experienced a marked lift in their fortunes. Others have not noticed the significant effects. There are numbers of up to date books on the subject. It is well worth investigating.

Like so many of the old techniques Feng Shui comes from

ancient China, where it may well have been possible to choose a site for your house and align the property, doors and windows etc. in the traditionally most propitious way. Obviously it is less possible to get everything right with regard to the house we live in today, but moving the furniture and possibly changing the use of one or two rooms has been known to have an effect.

Tassiography or the reading of tea cups, seems outmoded now and is thought of as being largely of gypsy origin. But in fact, it was also known in ancient China, where green tea was drunk from very distant times. It was also customary in Rome, where the dregs or grounds of the wine goblets were read and interpreted by the soothsayers, who would purport to see the future in them. The tea should be drunk, and the dregs moved by swirling the cup three times clockwise The handle is held towards the reader. Groups of tealeaves found on the left of the handle show events that are past. On the right, the future is found. Leaves near the bottom of the cup are further away in time than those near the rim. There are many groupings and symbols with traditional meanings.

Reading the pattern formed by clouds as they form and reform in the sky; or the leaping flames of a fire; the patterns in sand; the movements of birds; or even the fall of a leaf can all be used to advantage by those who are attuned to the idea that all is one, and that patterns formed here below are just a materialization of the patterns at a higher level.

Scrying is a Romany name for looking into a crystal ball. It takes a lot of practice to get results. Real or rock crystal balls are extremely expensive, but a fishermen's glass ball serves as a good substitute. They are used for crab and lobster pots and can sometimes be bought in seaside places. Look at the crystal in half darkness, not having any light falling directly on it. Concentrating quietly, you should eventually find the crystal appearing to go a bit 'milky'. Then, given time, pictures, scenes, faces, all sorts of apparitions can be seen in the crystal. You may have to make a good many attempts before you see anything. When you do, you will be left to interpret for yourself, what has appeared. It may have a dreamlike quality. You may never be quite certain whether it has 'reality' or has been produced by your own subconscious mind.

It is very common of course, for people to hope and even persuade themselves that they can see what the future holds by one or another of the many methods of divination. But in fact it seems to be only the principles involved that can really be seen, The understanding of the degree to which we have free will, and should use it, is often not acknowledged. This is the key to all the uses and abuses of divinatory methods.

Essentially, divination belongs to the realm of the psychic rather than the spiritual. We all love the psychic! But for the spiritual path, it does seem that work and effort to understand, are essential if there is to be any advancement through the years.

But there are also a range of practices, of which the use of the **pendulum** and the **dowsing rods** are good examples. These are the psychic skills, which are latent in all of us: the attributes of the psyche or soul, as distinct from spiritual understanding. Whether a pendulum on a cord swings, or a dowsing rod moves up and down apparently spontaneously in the hands of the practitioner, seems to depend on an impulse conveyed through the body to the hand. The source of the impulse may be deep in the mind or the heart, but if the practitioner is working honestly, it is not much influenced by the intellect. Of course, the intellect soon comes into play if you try to make the 'tool' move! But if you can relax with it, it appears to move of it own accord. It gives a 'yes' or 'no' answer to a question--or locates underground water, or hidden objects as the dowser walks over the ground.

Anyone can experiment. You can use a wedding ring on a thread if you haven't a pendulum. You can make dowsing rods out of wire coat hangers, as described elsewhere in this book. You may well feel a marked circular or back and forth swing in the pendulum, or a disconcertingly strong swing on the rods, which you know you aren't consciously directing.

You are your own Master

And yet something in you directs it, just as something in the master carpenter directs his tools so easily and smoothly, to give results that the apprentice doesn't get. Perhaps he puts his 'heart and soul' into the work under his hands. It's interesting that we speak of doing things with our whole heart and soul. We don't say 'I do it with my Spirit.' Instead we speak of 'entering into the spirit' of a thing, as though the Spirit is not under our command although the soul may be. It may be worth remembering Rodney Collin's idea that the soul can be 'wedded to the desires of the body, or to the aspirations of the Spirit.' It is possible that we can nurture, and consciously work, with the soul.

Each must make his/her own decision how to begin this work. If we have hesitated or drawn back time and again, bewildered and confused by the many conflicting opinions and apparently contradictory or discordant ideas that are thrust into the attention of the seeker, maybe George Elliot's idea, in the initial quotation at the beginning of this book, is worth considering. She is very conscious of the continual changeability of life: that all life is in eternal flux, as Heraclitus said. 'It is difficult to find any 'constant' to go by: the only constant is change.' So she mentions 'the element of tragedy that lies as the very heart of frequency.' And she felt that if we grew in consciousness, increasing sensitivity might lead us to 'die of that roar which lies at the other side of silence.' I think it is this subconscious 'roar' that often leads to fear of the unknown and unwillingness to look further. But there is probably nothing more fearful in the unknown than in the known world. We can only find a constant truth within our individual self. And listening quietly but intently, we may seem to deduce, as the roar subsides, a sweet sound, octave within octave of harmony, that calls us from The Other Side of Silence.

Suggested Exercises

1. What tools have you for practical use in the world? Your domestic and office tools for instance, and your tools of ordinary living and social intercourse?

2. What tools have you forged for yourself, for use in your emotional life and your relationships?

3. What about the spiritual tools? Do you keep the known ones clean and in good order? Is it time to look for finer ones?

4. Before laying this book aside, make a note of the chapter headings and run over in your mind the substance of any that were of particular interest to you.

5. Put this book on a shelf. Take leave of this friend who was first mentioned on P.2. And if you have a mind to, begin now to make a way forward for yourself again. A blessing on your endeavours!

The Magician

The sixteenth century Visconti Sforza deck designed by Bonefacio Bembo for the game of Tarocchi. This archetypal figure plays 'The Game of Life', using the basic tools: the pentacles or coins (earth) for worldly matters: the cups (water) for love, emotional or spiritual matters: the wand {fire} for ambition and aspiration: and the sword or knife (air) for aggression or assertiveness..

EPILOGUE

I have given a picture of an evolving world in an ever-changing, ever-developing universe.

I have indicated that all organisms on this earth, from the smallest and simplest living creature up to the much more complex level of mankind, are subject to and dependent on the fours elements that are available here: the earth and the mineral realm, the waters, the heat of the Sun without which the world would be a dark and lifeless place, and the mixture of gases which make up the air we can inhale and exhale safely.

I have then suggested that there is a fifth quality or element known to the ancients and variously called space or ether, which appears to sustain many discarnate beings as well as ourselves. We may recognise the idea of elemental beings-- elves, fairies etc. which are attached to this earthly world but not in fleshy form. And we may pay tribute to the higher worlds of Angels and Archangels which move freely about and beyond us.

I am suggesting that Mankind slots into Creation at a certain level, having feet on the earth and heads reaching towards the Heavens: and that our hearts and perhaps our souls may be drawn equally to both.

We are created in this half-way position, as the highest form of organic, or carnate life on this earth, and I find it possible that our purpose may be to bring the qualities of the Heavens, the spiritual qualities, to the earth, like conductors of electricity which transform or step current up or down: and in return, we may receive help to work our way back to our own source of Being, to the Godhead itself.

To fulfil this purpose, however, we need to be conscious of our own possibilities. To grow in consciousness we need to acquire the knowledge that Man is heir--to the knowledge struggled for and attained by our forebears down the many generations that have gone before. And remembering that by tradition we have also an Etheric Body, subject to the mysterious fifth element Space or Ether, which enables us to recognise and be recocognised by discarnate beings and possibly seek their help.

To seek for and be able to use the knowledge available to us is like learning to understand and use skilled tools. It takes time and effort.

But therein lies fulfilment.

Therein is the Way.

Bibliography

Baigent, Michael., Richard Leigh, and Henry Lincoln. *The Holy Blood and the Holy Grail*. London: Arrow, 1996.

Blum, Ralph. *The Book of Runes: a handbook for the use of an Ancient oracle, the Viking Runes*. 10th anniversary ed. New York: St.Martin's Press, 1993.

Blavatsky, H.P., *The Secret Doctrine: the synthesis of science, religion, and philosophy*. Facsimile ed. 2 vols. Pasadena: Theosophical University Press, 1999.

Bonewitz, R. A., and Lilian Verner Bonds. *New Cosmic Crystals*: *the ultimate course in crystal consciousness*. London: Thorsons,2000.

Case, E.M., *The Odour of Sanctity*. Crediton, Devon: privately printed. [1980's?].

Clement, Stephanie Jean. *What Astrology Can Do for You*. St. Paul, MN.: Llewellyn Publications,

Collin, Rodney. *The Theory of Celestial influence: man, the universe, and cosmic mystery*. Boulder: Shambhala, 1984.

-------. *The Theory of Eternal Life*. Boulder: Shambhala, 1984.

Copenhaver, Brian P., *Hermetica: The Greek Corpus Hermeticum and the Latin Asclepius in a New English Translation, With Notes And Introduction*.: Cambridge University Press, 1992.

Doyle, Arthur Conan. *The Coming of the Fairies*. London: Pavillion, 1997.

Du Maurier, George. *Peter Ibbetson*. London: Gollancz, 1969.

Dunne, John William. *An Experiment With Time.* Charlottesville, VA.: Hampton Roads Pub., 2001.

Gabirol, Solomon ben Judah Ibn. *The Fountain of Life: Fons Vitae.* Trans. Alfred B. Jacob. Stanwood, WA.: Sabian Pub. Society, 1987.

Govinda, Anagarika. *Foundations of Tibetan Mysticism.* York Beach,ME.: Red Wheel/Weiser, 1989.

Gurdjieff, Georges Ivanovitch. *Meetings With Remarkable Men.*
All and Everything, Second series. New York: Arkana/Penguin Books, 2000.

Hancock, Graham. *The Sign and The Seal: a quest for the lost Ark of the Covenant.* London: Arrow, 2001.

Harvey, Charles, and Suzi Harvey. *Thorsons Principles of Astrology.*London: Thorsons, 1999.

Mahesh Yogi, Maharishi. *Science of Being and Art of Living: Transcendental Meditation.* New York: Meridian, 1995.

Malory, Thomas. *Le Morte D'Arthur.* Ed. John Matthews. London: Cassell, 2000; distributed in the US by Sterling Pub. Co.

Ouspensky, P.D. *In Search of the Miraculous: fragments of an unknown teaching.* With a foreword by Marianne Williamson. San Diego,CA: Harcourt, Inc, 2001.

Pollack, Rachel. *Seventy-Eight Degrees of Wisdom: a book of Tarot.* Rev. ed. London: Thorsons, 1997.

Schlemmer, Phyllis V., and Palden Jenkins, compilers. *The*

Only Planet of Choice: essential briefings from deep space. With a foreword by John Whitmore. Bath: Gateway, 1993.

Steiner, Rudolf. *How to Know Higher Worlds: the classic guide to the spiritual journey.* Trans. Christopher Bamford. Great Barrington,MA: Anthroposophic Press, 2002.

Sumohadiwidjojo, Muhammad Subuh. *Susila Budhi Dharma.* 3rd rev. Ed. Rickmansworth, England: Subud Publications, 1991.

Underwood, Guy. *The Pattern of the Past.* New York:Abelard- Schuman, 1973.

Watkins, Alfred. The Old Straight Track. London: Abacus, 1987.

Index

Abraham 187
Adams, John Couch 45–6
air element 34, 36
Aldwick (carpenter) 200
ancient stones *see* standing stones
angelic grace 71
angelic kingdom 69
angels 69–78
angled stones 127–8
animal trackways 122–3
animals 43, 122, 123
Apollo 170
Aquarian Age 181, 183–4
Aquarius 173
Arcana 150
archangels 69–78
Arian Age 182
Aries 172
Ark of the Covenant 187–8
Assiah 194
astrology 37, 164–85
automatic pilot 6–7
awareness 14, 142
Aziluth 194

Batons (Tarot) 160
beginner's mind 2–3
Bembo, Bonifacio 150, 157, 211
Binah (understanding) 191
black arts 99
Blavatsky, H.P. 5, 58, 79
blind springs 121, 122, 124
Blum, Ralph 205
Bonewitz, Ra 11–12, 24–5
brain 5
Briah 194

Cabala 186
Cancer 172
Cancerian Age 182

Capricorn 173
Case, Enid 96
cataleptic trances 111–12
Cathars 56
caution 67, 91
chakras 62–7
chance 149
change 141
channelling 80–2
Chariot (Tarot) 154
cheirology 36–7, 204
churches 118, 121–2, 123–4, 128
Clement, Stephanie J. 185
Clubs (Tarot) 160, 161
Coins (Tarot) 160, 161
Collin, Rodney
  consciousness, growth in 145
  Florentine Academy 59
  Four Worlds 194
  soul 42, 209
  study programme 132
  Theory of Celestial Influence 58, 60
colour 24, 65
Column of Force 190
Column of Form 190
Conan Doyle, Sir Arthur 40, 41
conkers 30
consciousness, growth of 3, 33, 91, 145
Cook, Captain 93
Cottingley fairies 40–1
crystals 18–32
  working with 25–8
Cups (Tarot) 160, 161

Daat (knowledge) 191
daisies 43
Death (Tarot) 156
Deer Stone, Glendalough 126

217

Devil (Tarot) 157
discipline 48, 140, 142
divas 39
dowsing 118, 121, 129–30, 208
Doyle, Sir Arthur Conan 40, 41
dreams 104–5, 107–11
   lucid 108–11
   time 113–15
Dunne, John 113–14

earth element 33, 36
education 50
elemental kingdoms 28
elementals 39
elements 11, 33–7
elephants 123
Elliot, George 209
elves 38–9
emotions, negative 7–8, 15
Emperor (Tarot) 153
Empress (Tarot) 153
energy 3–4
   free 22–5
   leaks 7–8, 15
energy fields 101–2
esoteric knowledge 4–5
esoteric school 50–3
ether 33, 34, 36
evocation 87
extrasensory experience 98–100

fairies 38–41
feng shui 206–7
Ficcino, Marcilio 59
field boundaries 124
fire element 33, 36
First Cause 3–4
Fool (Tarot) 152
forest ponies 122
Four Worlds 194–6
free will 10
Freemasons 50, 51, 123–4, 128

Gabirol, Solomon ben 88

Gabriel 72, 75
Gaia 11, 48
gaming cards 159–61
Gemini 172
Geminian Age 182
geodetic lines 120, 121, 124
Gevura (judgement) 191
Glastonbury Zodiac 129
gnomes 38–9
Govinda, Anagarika 205
Great Ages 181–3
Griffiths, Frances 40
guides 78–85
Gurdjieff, G.I. 6, 58, 135, 137

Halevi, Z'ev ben Shimon 74, 190–1, 198
Hancock, Graham 188
hand reading 36–7, 204
Hanged Man (Tarot) 156
Haniel 72
Harvey, Charles and Suzi 185
healing, crystals 26–7
hearing 94–5
hearing voices 100
Heirophant (Tarot) 153
heresies 58
Hermetica 54
Hermit (Tarot) 155
Hesed (mercy) 191
High Priest (Tarot) 153
High Priestess (Tarot) 153
higher self 84, 110
Hochma (wisdom) 191
Hod (reverberation) 191
horoscopes 174–7
horse chestnuts 30
Houses (horoscope chart) 174–5
hypnogogia 105, 106–8
hypnopompia 105
hypnosis 107

I Ching 203–4
imagination 44–6

inceptional charts 180
individuals 61
initiation ceremonies 552–3
intelligence 33, 42–4
invocation 87

Jenkins, Palden 77
Jerusalem 50
Judgement (Tarot) 158–9
Jung, C.G. 164
Jupiter 169
Justice (Tarot) 155

Kenton, Warren *see* Halevi, Z'ev ben Shimon
Kether (Crown) 190, 191
Knights Hospitallers 51
Knights of St John of Jerusalem 51
Knights Templar 52
Kundalini energy 66

Leary, Timothy 105, 110, 111
Leo 172
Leonian Age 182
Lethbridge, T.C. 119
ley lines 116–18, 122, 128
Libra 172–3
light 19–20
Lightning Flash 192–4
love 4
Lover (Tarot) 154
lucid dreaming 108–11
lunar cults 120–2
lych gates 124

Magician (Tarot) 152, 211
Maharishi Mahesh Yogi 5, 45, 98, 109
Major Arcana cards 150, 152–9
Malkut (Kingdom) 190, 191, 192, 194, 195
Maltwood, Mrs 129
mankind 31–2

Mars 169
Mary Line 118, 128
maternal role 49
Maurier, Georges du 108
Medici, Cosimo di 59
Medici, Lorenzo de 59
meditation 106, 112
Medjugorje 67
Melchizedek 187
Mercury 169
Metatron 73
Michael 72, 75
Michael Line 117–18, 128
Michell, John 117
mineral kingdom 11–12, 20, 22, 29
Minor Arcana cards 150, 159–61
Moon 171
Moon (Tarot) 158

negative emotions 7–8, 15
Neo-Platonic Academy 58–9
Neptune 170
Netzah (eternity) 191
numbers 131–8
numerology 205–6
nymphs 39

objectives, achieving 139–41
occult knowledge 4–5, 53–4
octaves, law of 135–9
organic life 31, 42
Origen 57
Ouspensky, P.D. 14

pagodas 36
Paracelsus 38
paternal role 49
Pelagius 57
pendulums 208
Pentacles (Tarot) 160, 161
philosophy 9
Piscean Age 182

219

Pisces 173–4
planets 169–71
plants 30, 31, 42, 43
Pluto 170
Pollack, Rachel 163
ponies, forest 122
Pope (Tarot) 153
power 99
Prieuré de Sion 55–6
Ptolemy 181
pysche 42
Pythagoras 11, 90, 205

Raphael 72, 75
Raziel 73
reality, nature of 108
recumbent stones 126
Red Cross 52
Rollright Stones 125
runes 204-5
Rydell, Catherine 80–1, 82, 85, 86, 110

Sagittarius 173
salamanders 39
Samael 72–3
Sandolphon 72
Saturn 169
Schlemmer, Phyllis 77, 80
School Men 55, 57
Scorpio 173
scrying 207–8
secret doctrine 55–7
self discipline 49, 142
self-remembering 12–16
self-understanding 3
senses 13–14
    working with 90–103
Sephiroth *see* Stations of the Tree
seven 134
sight 92–4
sleep 104–5
smell 95–7

Society for the Study of Spiritual Science 80
space *see* ether
spirit 38
spirit mentors, invoking 82–5
spiritual tools 100–1, 145–6, 177, 201–3
St John Ambulance 52
standing stones 118–19, 120, 125–8
Star (Tarot) 157
Stations of the Tree 190–2
Staves (Tarot) 160
Steiner, Rudolf 1–2, 58, 183
stone circles *see* standing stones
Stonehenge 126–7, 127–8
Strength (Tarot) 154–5
subtlety within 177–9
Subuh, Pak 96
Sun 170
Sun (Tarot) 158
supersensory experience 95–8
Sutton, Lou 111
Swords (Tarot) 160, 161
sylphs 39

Tarot 145–63
tassiography 207
taste 98
Taurean Age 182
Taurus 172
Teilhard de Chardin 20, 96
Temperance (Tarot) 156
Tepheret (beauty) 191, 193, 195
third force 133–5
Thom, Alexander 119
Thoth 146–7
time 164
    in dreams 113–15
tools, spiritual 100–1, 145–6, 177, 201–3
touch 97
Tower of Destruction (Tarot) 157

220

trances 87, 106
  cataleptic 111–12
Tree of Life 186–98
Trevelyan, Sir George 18
twelve 134

Underwood, Guy 118, 120–2
undines 39
Uranus 170, 184
Uriel 75

Venus 169
Virgo 172
voices, hearing 100

Wands (Tarot) 160, 161
water diviners 118
water element 33, 36
Watkins, Alfred 116–17
Webb, James 58
Wheels of Fortune (Tarot) 155
White Eagle Lodge 79–80
White, Ruth 79
will 142
World (Tarot) 159
Wright, Elsie 40

Yesod (Foundation) 191, 194
Yetzirah 194

Zadkiel 73
Zaphkiel 73
Zodiac
  Glastonbury 129
  signs of 37, 166–8, 171–4

Printed in the United Kingdom
by Lightning Source UK Ltd.
9718200001B/169-228